D0187068

FIVE GOOD IDEAS

PRACTICAL STRATEGIES FOR NON-PROFIT SUCCESS

Edited by ALAN BROADBENT *and* RATNA OMIDVAR

Coach House Books, Toronto

Copyright © the contributors, 2011

First edition

Canada Council   Conseil des Arts   ONTARIO ARTS COUNCIL   Canadä
for the Arts   du Canada   CONSEIL DES ARTS DE L'ONTARIO

Published with the generous assistance of the Canada Council for the Arts and the
Ontario Arts Council. Coach House Books also acknowledges the support of the
Government of Canada through the Canada Book Fund and the Government of
Ontario through the Ontario Book Publishing Tax Credit.

LIBRARY AND ARCHIVES CANADA CATALOGUING IN PUBLICATION

Five good ideas : practical strategies for non-profit success / edited by Alan Broadbent
and Ratna Omidvar.

Includes bibliographical references and index.
ISBN 978-1-55245-246-2

1. Nonprofit organizations – Management.
I. Broadbent, Alan II. Omidvar, Ratna

HD62.6.F58 2011   658'.048   C2011-906033-7

 MAYTREE
For Leaders. For Change.

Five Good Ideas is a Maytree initiative.
The opinions expressed in this book are those of the authors
and do not necessarily represent those of Maytree.

Five Good Ideas: Practical Strategies for Non-Profit Success
is also available as an ebook (978 1 177056 303 2).

CONTENTS

Foreword *by Craig Kielburger* / vii

Introduction *by Alan Broadbent* / xi

1 Leadership and Vision

Reimagining Your Organization · NICK SAUL / 3

Leadership · ROCCO ROSSI / 10

Institutional Change · ALOK MUKHERJEE / 16

Influencing Change · JOHN OESCH / 23

Strategic Planning · JAMES APPLEYARD / 27

Turning Your Organization Around · PAUL DAVIDSON / 33

Innovation · SUZANNE GIBSON / 38

2 Organizational Effectiveness

Leading an Inclusive Organization · KAY BLAIR / 45

Shared Services · SHARON B. COHEN / 49

Managing Risk · DEREK BALLANTYNE / 53

Not-for-Profit Corporations Law · SHEILA CRUMMEY / 59

Dealing with a Large-Scale Emergency · THOMAS APPLEYARD / 66

3 Human Resources

Effective HR Management · LYNNE TOUPIN / 77

Improving Employment Relations · DAVE MCKECHNIE / 84

Managing Union Relations · FRANCES LANKIN / 91

Working with Volunteers · GAIL NYBERG / 97

Managing Consultant Relationships · DAVID PECAUT / 102

4   Resource Development

Financial Management · LOIS FINE / 111

Translating Vision into Funding · PAUL BORN / 118

Approaching Grantmakers Successfully · ROBIN CARDOZO / 122

Corporate Fundraising · SUSAN McISAAC / 127

Fundraising for Small and Medium-sized
   Organizations · ROSS McGREGOR / 132

Developing Resources Through Partnerships · HELEN WALSH / 138

5   Communications

Branding · IAN CHAMANDY & KEN ABER / 147

Strategic Communications · JENNIFER LYNN / 153

Maximized Marketing for Non-Profits · DONNIE CLAUDINO / 157

Social Marketing · MARK SARNER / 162

Talking to the Media · CAROL GOAR / 167

Web 2.0 · JASON MOGUS / 175

Building Conversations on the Web ·
   MARCO CAMPANA & CHRISTOPHER WULFF / 183

Successful Networking · LISA MATTAM / 190

6   Advocacy and Policy

Government Relations · JUDY PFEIFER / 197

Advocacy · SEAN MOORE / 204

Working with Government Budgets · DAN BURNS / 212

Impacting Public Policy · BENJAMIN PERRIN / 218

7   Governance

Managing Board–Executive Director
   Relationships · RICK POWERS / 227

Board Governance · TOM WILLIAMS / 232

Diversifying your Board · MAYTREE / 237

Acknowledgements / 247

The Editors / 248

FOREWORD

by Craig Kielburger

I STILL remember the April morning in 1995 when I stood nervously in front of my Grade 7 class holding a crumpled newspaper article about child labour.

'I don't know what, but we have to do something,' I said. 'Who will join?'

Eleven hands shot up. Free The Children was born.

I've found in retelling this story that it's usually the 'Who will join?' part and the 11 hands that grab people's attention. But when I look back, what strikes me most is the first half of my statement: I meant it when I said I didn't know what to do. I wasn't out to start a charity – none of us were. Heck, we hadn't yet tackled high school math, let alone finance, international development and selecting a board of directors. We just wanted to help.

After our initial enthusiasm, few opportunities emerged for us young people to get involved beyond handing over our parents' credit cards. So we started Free The Children and led ourselves straight up a steep learning curve. In retrospect, it felt more like a learning *cliff.*

The cliffs that exist within the non-profit world can often seem insurmountable. In a sector that relies largely on pro bono work, donations and sheer passion, you're expected to take on a lot of tasks corporations would normally hire out. But once you overcome the initial fear, the incredible part of the non-profit sector emerges – the part with the wealth of brilliant minds and innovative thinkers willing to give you a boost.

Looking back, our little group had an advantage in being so young. It was natural that we asked for help – that's what we did in class. More than that, the experts we contacted didn't expect us to have all the answers. They appreciated our eagerness to learn, and that increased their willingness to teach.

Aside from experts, we also received advice from the people in our communities around the world – the very people we were trying to help. By listening to them, we learned one of our first lessons in influencing change.

After finally raising enough money to build our first school in Kenya, we were ecstatic when the walls went up. But that excitement turned to disappointment when we saw a problem – no girls came to the newly built classroom. Searching for a solution, we looked to the community elders. They explained that the lack of girls had nothing to do with culture. It's just that young women didn't have time for school when they needed to collect water.

That statement was the first part of a long lesson. We weren't development specialists, but we learned from our conversation that we couldn't lift people out of poverty – we had to help them lift themselves.

Slowly we broadened our scope. Wells became the second phase of our plan. Phase two turned into three and then four as health care and alternative income became clear necessities in achieving sustainability. That became the basis of our Adopt a Village model, which is now active in hundreds of communities in seven countries.

As our organization grew, we saw the value of the knowledge others in our field were gaining. We were inspired by innovative groups like Stephen Lewis's Grandmothers to Grandmothers campaign and Zainab Salbi's Women for Women International, which looked beyond high-net-worth donors to facets of our society that wanted to help but weren't traditionally targeted. These markets can be powerful. Today, about 55 percent of Free The Children's funding comes from youth.

Once we recognized the power of young people, we wanted others to see it too. That desire became the basis for We Day, an annual event that brings 70,000 young people together in five stadiums across Canada to celebrate the work they've done and learn how they can continue making a difference. This free event is broadcast as a prime-time CTV special. To get tickets, youth are required to take one local and one global action.

As a result, young We Day participants annually log over 1 million volunteer hours and raise millions of dollars for more than 500 charities across the country. Instead of competing with other non-profits, this event has allowed us to encourage the growth of the next generation of philanthropists supporting a spectrum of causes.

These young people have us excited about what's to come.

We're beginning to see an incredible shift in focus, with the non-profit sector embracing social enterprise. For too long, charities have competed for the same 5 to 10 percent – that's the portion of income or time the average person can donate to charity. In young people especially, we see a desire to have a positive impact with the other 90 to 95 percent of our income and time – what we eat, what we wear and how we spend money.

One of the people leading this emerging field of social enterprise is Jeff Skoll, the founding president of eBay. When the Canadian businessman left the internet behemoth, he started seeking out other vehicles for change. He founded a film company called Participant Media to make movies with a message, and scored big with Al Gore's *An Inconvenient Truth*.

With the mentorship of Jeff and other innovators, we were able to form Me to We, a Canadian social enterprise that provides consumers with sweatshop-free organic clothes, socially conscious books, volunteer trips and youth-leadership training experiences. These choices and programs give people the opportunity to create change every day. With half of Me to We's profits donated to Free The Children and the other half reinvested into the social enterprise to continue its growth, we can ensure that the bottom line is measured not in dollars earned, but instead in the positive social impact we make.

I think of this book much like the early advisors and mentors who fostered Free The Children and Me to We's development. The success of everyone in the non-profit world and the emerging social-enterprise sector is dependent on the sharing of information, ideas and experiences.

Both this book and the Maytree lunch-and-learn program provide an important exchange of ideas to guide us as we collectively embark up another steep learning curve.

This knowledge is not meant to help any one group – it's about strengthening the whole. By collecting the expertise of people who have forged this trail before us, we can set about scaling new cliffs and bettering the world.

INTRODUCTION

by Alan Broadbent

GOOD MANAGEMENT is based on the ability to put good ideas into action. Whether one is running a business, a community organization, a government department, a school or a hospital, putting good ideas into action is critical to success.

The idea for this book arose in 2003 when I returned from a two-day conference and compared notes with my colleague Ratna Omidvar, Maytree president, who had returned from a similar conference. Asking our usual question of each other – 'Did you learn anything useful for our work?' – we ascertained that my conference, unfortunately, had produced a rather low yield, one middling idea, and hers had produced two. We then began to wonder if taking time to attend conferences was worth it.

Of course, there are benefits to conferences that have more to do with networking and relationships than content, but when we attend conferences for two or three days, the volume of work crossing our desks doesn't abate. When we're back in the office, we face today's work, plus that of the days we missed.

Admittedly, we were both feeling a little conference – and road – weary.

So we began to imagine how great it would be to obtain the benefits of a conference without having to actually attend. And if we could do that, how about striving for multiple benefits? Instead of getting one good idea in two days, how about getting two in one day? Heavens, why stop there – how about five good ideas over lunch? At that moment, we stopped, looked at each other and launched the Five Good Ideas series.

Over the past eight years, Maytree has hosted lunch-and-learn sessions on a wide range of management-related topics. The topics result from our ongoing canvass of people working in community-sector organizations. We ask them a simple question: what do you need to know to help you run your organization better? Some of the answers are obvious, like fundraising, information technology and governance. Others are less so, like managing in a unionized environment, branding and planning for emergencies such as an epidemic or earthquake.

The formula is simple. We ask leading experts and practitioners in each topic area to make a presentation. They do it with enthusiasm and without compensation, and we make them work! Rather than give a 'canned' presentation, we ask that they frame their advice as Five Good Ideas they feel will make people think and act better. We don't want a survey course on, say, fundraising; rather, we are looking for those Five Good Ideas that people can take back to the office, share with colleagues and apply to their work. (We've been asked why we don't call them Five Great Ideas, because many of them clearly are great ideas, but we had a little modesty spasm and opted for understatement.)

At each session, the presenter speaks for 20 minutes, after which the participants (seated at round tables of about ten people) discuss the topic for another 20 minutes. This lively discussion also serves as a networking opportunity that often connects the most unlikely partners, and is followed by a chance for participants to question, challenge or seek clarification from the speaker, as well as share their own experience on the topic.

Five Good Ideas is an inexpensive program for Maytree to run. We rent Elmsley Hall on the University of Toronto campus, which has a wall of windows giving on to a lovely terrace garden, beautiful all year round. We provide a bag lunch of a sandwich, an apple and a drink, and request that people RSVP, but we do not charge a fee. We record the session and place a summary with video on the Maytree website (http://www.maytree.com) for those who may have missed the session or wish to share or revisit it.

We have had people from many parts of the community sector attend, usually 80 to 100 per session. While our initial target audience was from Maytree's granting cohort in the anti-poverty and immigrant and refugee settlement fields, it quickly grew beyond that to include people from all kinds of community organizations, including the arts, health care and education, sports and recreation, and many other areas. We even attract people from the business and political communities.

Good management is important everywhere. But it is especially important in the community sector, which operates with much complexity, often high stress and few resources. The sector is thinly managed, so the people who are there have to be good at many things – and good pretty well all the time. Community-sector leaders must wear a variety of hats, as their organizations don't enjoy the luxury of many specialized management positions.

At Maytree we have a great respect for how well the sector is managed, particularly under constrained circumstances. We are also aware of the high degree of innovation in the sector, often a result of necessity. Five Good Ideas is a way for sector leaders to begin to think about the important elements of the range of skills they must perform. They rarely have the luxury of time to dive deeply into each area, but they can be well-served by being exposed to what some of the best thinkers and practitioners consider the top ideas. The Five Good Ideas.

1

LEADERSHIP
AND VISION

SUCCESSFULLY REIMAGINING a non-profit organization isn't simple. Part determination, part optimism and part good fortune, the process requires a great board and staff, a lot of strategic listening, a willingness to take risks, and relentless incrementalism – for all change takes time.

– Nick Saul

REIMAGINING YOUR ORGANIZATION

Nick Saul

1 Listen

2 Create a plan (but don't always stick to it)

3 Embrace your inner entrepreneur

4 Remember: it's competitive out there

5 Contribute to public policy conversations; don't get swallowed up by service delivery

SUCCESSFULLY REIMAGINING A non-profit organization isn't simple. Part determination, part optimism and part good fortune, the process requires a great board and staff, a lot of strategic listening, a willingness to take risks, and relentless incrementalism – for all change takes time.

When I arrived at The Stop in 1998, it was a straightforward food bank: three staff members in a small space, a few programs and a very modest budget. Today we're a full-fledged community food centre with 35 to 40 staff, two locations, multiple programs and a budget ten times what it once was.

There was no silver bullet, no 'miracle grow' that got us there. But there are some ideas we've refined along the way that help articulate our approach to change.

1 Listen

It sounds obvious, but it isn't easy to pull off. Listening isn't just a matter of sending out feelers once every four years when you put together a strategic plan: it needs to be habitual, part of your organizational DNA. You listen to be relevant and responsive, and also because it demonstrates that you value people and their ideas, that members of your community have something to say and that you're willing to listen. Organizations that listen well feel and look very different than those that don't.

At the beginning of The Stop's reinvention we did a lot of listening: to partner organizations, funders, staff and – most importantly – the community, the people who walked through our doors on a regular basis. Since then we've held community dinners, hosted impromptu town

☛ **Creating The Stop's Plan**

When we reached out to the community, we heard that food banks simply aren't enough, and so we focused our efforts on using food to build health, community, environmental sustainability and greater equity. We listened to gain a better sense of our goal (to provide a more comprehensive approach to food security) and then evaluated various programs and strategies to determine how we could pursue that goal most effectively.

halls, issued an annual survey, conducted focused conversations with community leaders and noted the day-to-day feedback staff receive as they deliver services.

That last point is essential: staff need to be open to hearing both the good and the bad, and have mechanisms for relaying that feedback to the organizational leadership – through staff meetings, reports, logs, year-end program evaluations and so on. Pay particular attention to your team's own feedback as well. Create space for the generation of new ideas and for discussion: encourage staff to walk into your office, take time to solicit comments at staff meetings, make an open-ended conversation part of your annual board-staff retreat. Good ideas are lurking everywhere.

Still, not every idea is a good one; as a leader you need a plan, something that will filter and rein in the many suggestions that are out there. Which brings us to . . .

2 Create a plan (but don't always stick to it)

Listening followed up with honest evaluation is what produces a plan. A SWOT analysis (strengths, weaknesses, opportunities, threats) of all the feedback and ideas you receive will help you create a roadmap that is clear – for both internal and external purposes – about your goals and the initiatives that will best help you meet them.

Make your plan fairly broad, because you'll need room to manoeuvre, to tweak and refine your implementation, within the broad aims that you set. Also, remember that plans are important, but they are never perfect: a plan is always a work in progress. Don't get so caught up in making your plan that you stall before taking action, and don't let the perfect be the enemy of the good.

Your plan needs to be *yours* – this is one thing you cannot outsource. While you might hire an outside consultant to help facilitate your planning process, at the end of the day you need to write your plan yourself and fully own it. Because your plan will inform your organization's entire development, this is one area you really want to micromanage. And once your plan is written, make it public. It'll help clarify your activities for your stakeholders and community members. (I am always surprised at how few organizations do this.)

When you start to implement your plan, something interesting is going to happen: you'll start to say no to things and feel good about that, because you'll know *why* you're saying no. You'll have clarity of purpose and direction, and that will enable you to make smart choices.

3 Embrace your inner entrepreneur

Non-profits need to be as opportunistic and nimble as possible: the landscape in which you are delivering services can shift quickly, and unforeseen opportunities will arise. You must be willing to be bold and think big.

Non-profits need to be as opportunistic and nimble as possible.

At The Stop, our biggest moment of boldness came with the investment in the Green Barn: a full-service food facility that includes a greenhouse, kitchen, classroom and office space. We recognized that it was a calculated risk, but we embraced it – we did our homework and concluded that the Green Barn was an incredible opportunity, one we couldn't afford to miss. It was too good a chance to put our food work on the map and to create a bigger platform to tell our story. We felt strongly that it would attract the attention, people and resources required to pull it off.

Key to making the decision – and raising the $5 million we needed – was a keen understanding of the cultural context in which we were operating. The good-food revolution was on, and people were starting to think and ask questions about food like never before. This was one entrepreneurial element: recognizing that the conditions were ripe for the acceptance of our project.

The heightened awareness around food has also helped fuel our social enterprise initiatives, enabling us to reach into wealthier communities through our dinners, cookbook, farmers' market and catering. Along with raising our profile, most of this activity is focused on generating our own funds and then driving them back into our mission.

A spur to our entrepreneurialism has also been our funding model, which is largely based on private donations. This leaves us little choice but to always be in action mode, finding new ways to come at issues, get our story out, reach for new audiences. While I think you need a good balance between government funding (which is stable but prescriptive, since money is often earmarked for specific programs) and private support (which can be fickle but often flexible), the private element is important and has been essential to The Stop's innovation and growth.

4 Remember: it's competitive out there

This is perhaps the elephant in the room. Obviously you never want to run another organization down, and you should always give kudos where they are due, but you must also be able to differentiate yourself from others, be clear about the difference your organization is making and why you have no equals in the pursuit of your mission.

It isn't just a question of having solid programming – you must then be good at telling your story, and feel comfortable 'selling' what you do.

One important aspect of this: you need to be known. There are many people who have the capacity to help your organization, but they need to be familiar with it first. It's imperative to get out from behind your desk, and you should schedule this time. When the Rotary Club, local church or local cable station ask you to speak – speak! And if they don't ask, tell them why you'd be a great person to invite.

Be relentless in seeking out fundraising opportunities. Create a good database to track donations, research potential contributors and make sure your organization looks and sounds professional so you can appeal to them convincingly. Hire a photographer; write polished copy; use newsletters and annual reports to communicate your successes; engage your community via social media. Your approach to these details matters.

And before you're left with the impression that I am a craven capitalist, I'll get to my final point . . .

5 Contribute to public policy conversations; don't get swallowed up by service delivery

We're all in the non-profit sector to change the social goal posts, to create a more progressive and equitable world. We therefore need to address the systemic changes that must take place to bring this about. After all, social change can't happen within the confines of a single organization.

Hire active, politically minded staff, and populate your board with people who share your values and an interest in creating greater equity. Create time for your staff to be involved in community groups, networks and coalitions. In your communications, always link your front-line experiences to broader social challenges in order to illustrate what needs changing. Most importantly, support your community's efforts to speak out on the issues that matter most to it.

Support your community's efforts to speak out on the issues that matter most to it.

Don't be scared of advocacy. It doesn't turn people off; rather, it makes you relevant. Obviously you need to be strategic about the way you advocate – you certainly don't want to be shrill or partisan. But engaging with public policy helps create a culture in which your organization sees itself – and is seen by others – as part of larger-scale solutions, and not just operating within the confines of a specific community.

**FIVE GOOD
RESOURCES**

1. Anything by urban visionary Jane Jacobs or by master listener Studs Terkel, best known for his oral histories such as *Hard Times: An Oral History of the Great Depression* (Pantheon, 1986).

2. Carve out some time to recharge your batteries by watching the innovative people and big ideas at TED Talks: http://www.ted.com/talks.

3. http://www.grassrootsfundraising.org and http://www.charityinfo.ca for good tips and straightforward advice on fundraising and communication.

4. Every organization needs a compass for its work. Janet Poppendieck's *Sweet Charity? Emergency Food and the End of Entitlement* (Penguin, 1998) has helped guide my own work.

5. *Norma Rae*, starring Sally Field (1979). It's an inspiring movie about drawing a line in the sand and standing up for what you believe in.

As executive director of The Stop Community Food Centre for many years, **NICK SAUL** has built the organization into an international leader in the fight to eradicate hunger and to create healthier, self-sufficient and sustainable communities. He and Stop staff have pioneered an innovative new model in the community food centre, where healthy food and universal access to it is seen not as a privilege but as a basic human right. Nick is currently working on the development of a new umbrella organization to promote the resourcing and development of new community food centres in Canada. He has also worked at several other non-profits, in government and in the labour movement. Nick is a Queen's Golden Jubilee Medal winner for significant contribution to Canada and community (2002), the recipient of the Jane Jacobs Prize (2008) and the proud father of two young boys.

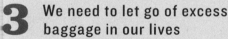 **LEADERSHIP**

Rocco Rossi

1 Focus on the journey,
not the destination

2 A journey of a thousand kilometres
begins with one step

3 We need to let go of excess
baggage in our lives

4 Never underestimate the generosity
of other people nor the pleasure
of providing service to others

5 Being alone is not the same
as being lonely

GIVE YOURSELF PERMISSION to be selfish. I believe, deeply, that if you're going to renew yourself as a leader and have the energy you need to lead people in your organization, you have to be selfish. It's much like when you're in an airplane and the flight attendant says, 'In case of depressurization, an oxygen mask will drop down. Make sure you reach for the oxygen and put your own mask on before attempting to help others.'

All of us, in one way or another, are searching for our source of oxygen.

The need for renewal among leaders is more pressing today than at any other time in history because of the accelerating pace of change, which is putting great pressures on both material and human capacities in all segments of society. We all need more oxygen.

I have been in a hurry from the time I was born. I was in a hurry to get through school, to become a VP, to buy the biggest house and the best car I could. I was fortunate, and things came my way. I was able to transfer academic success into business success. I thought that I pretty much had it made. I possessed all of the things I was supposed to have at a very young age. But then I got a huge wake-up call.

I was at Labatt's at the time, working as senior vice-president. The CEO, Don Kitchen, and I were visiting our board in Belgium, as the company was about to go public. We had put some pieces in place that made that change possible, decisions that would make all of us very wealthy – you can imagine the huge celebration.

We were to have breakfast the next morning, but Don died in his sleep of a massive coronary, at age 44. The very first event in the house that he and his wife, Linda, had spent two and a half years renovating was his wake.

I found myself incapable of staying at my job, but I wasn't sure what I would do next. After some travelling, and another work stint that proved dispiriting, I went on what I think of as my real-life MBA: I walked the Camino de Santiago in Spain.

The Camino is a Christian pilgrimage that was established in the mid-800s when a hermit discovered the remains of St. James the Greater, an apostle of Christ and the first to be martyred. St. James had been beheaded and his body, legend has it, was spirited away to Spain and found by this hermit in Santiago.

The Camino journey can start in different parts of Europe; I decided to do the Camino Francés, which is the route inside Spain. You stay in monasteries and church basements and hostels along the way, and meet the most extraordinary people. Most importantly, there is a chance to reflect in silence and quiet – something that, as a society, we have few opportunities to do.

Out of this experience, I distilled some ideas.

1 Focus on the journey, not the destination

When you make the pilgrimage to Rome or to Jerusalem, it's all about the destination: walking in the footsteps of Christ along the Via Dolorosa, seeing where the martyrs are buried in St. Peter's. The Camino de Santiago, by contrast, is about the time you spend along the way – what matters are the thoughts, development, prayers, laughter, crying and the rest that you do on the journey. In this sense, the Camino is similar to what we do each and every day in our work.

The one person who put this into stark relief for me was a fellow pilgrim named Jesús, a youth counsellor from Malaga. He had spent the better part of 18 years, day in and day out, counselling at-risk youth who had abused substances, abused others or been abused themselves. And then he woke up one day and realized he couldn't solve the problems of every youth in Malaga. He was overwhelmed, despairing. He couldn't do his job anymore.

It was amazing to meet Jesús 500 kilometres later in another town – ready to go back to Malaga. He had come to realize the power of those he had reached and saved, and this helped to renew his energy as a leader.

Large goals are important – they're necessary for forward motion – but they cannot overwhelm the experience of what you are doing on a day-to-day basis, or the value of what you accomplish in those days.

2 A journey of a thousand kilometres begins with one step

It's an old cliché, and it's a cliché for a reason: there is a powerful truth to it. It's good to have ambitions, but it is also easy to be overwhelmed by them. When we take a problem or mission and break it down into individual steps, it is incredible what we can and do achieve.

Nine hundred kilometres is roughly the distance between Toronto and Quebec City. If any one of us were to turn to our friends or family and say, 'Well, I'm just going for a walk to Quebec City,' they'd think we were nuts. People don't walk to Quebec City – they take a plane, a train or a car. And yet, the walk can be achieved – step by step by step. Break down those problems, goals and challenges into manageable portions.

3 We need to let go of excess baggage in our lives

The third idea is drawn from two key symbols on the Camino: the backpack and stones.

Each and every night, a pilgrim finds herself going through a reassessment of what is in her backpack to determine what is actually necessary for the journey, and what she can do without. Along the Camino there are piles of discarded clothing, left by people deciding, 'I don't need that fourth shirt. I don't need that sixth pair of pants. I really don't want any excess weight because that is not going to help me get where I want to go. In fact, it's causing my blisters, it's causing my pain.' We carry a lot of literal and metaphorical baggage with us, and it causes us pain.

Beyond the backpack is the story of the stones. Two-thirds of the way across the Camino there is a wonderful place called the Cruz de Ferro, which is a large iron cross at the top of a hill. At the base of the cross is a massive cairn of pebbles and stones: 30 feet in diameter, 20 feet high, literally millions of rocks that vary in size from the tip of your pinky to four and five pounds. Each of these pebbles and stones has been carried by a pilgrim, in some cases hundreds or thousands of kilometres. During the walk, pilgrims consider the mental baggage they are carrying: some have painful childhood memories, others have moments of harshness, some are burdened by acts of their own, others by words said by another. Pilgrims spend the time leading up to the Cruz de Ferro working that pain into the stone, and at the cross they drop their stone, leaving their pain with it.

Each of us must learn to let go of excess baggage, both mental and material, because it detracts from the energy we need in order to lead.

4 Never underestimate the generosity of other people nor the pleasure of providing service to others

Along the Camino I met a wonderful woman in a rundown town in the Meseta, a very dry, poor part of northern Spain. She provided me with food and water and directions to a building I wanted to see. At the end of our meeting she said, 'No, no. I don't want any payment. When you get to Santiago, pray for me. My name is Gloria.'

As your journey progresses, you become a champion for other people.

Each of us, every single day, is a champion for a community. Sometimes this means we do things that other people cannot do for themselves – but we also receive so much. It is important to re-energize your spirit to take on the challenges you face. Finding joy in the work and in your relationship to your community is essential.

5 Being alone is not the same as being lonely

The fifth idea is one that we in the West have a tremendous amount of difficulty dealing with: the notion that being alone is not the same as being lonely. The only times I've ever been lonely in my life have been in crowds. Loneliness means being surrounded by people with whom you have nothing in common.

Being deliberately alone, however, allows you to find stillness. Stillness is the source of oxygen from which we can draw refreshment. In our modern, frenzied world, stillness is under such attack that we have no time to touch the divine – whatever that means to each of us – because we're trying to get through an incredible cacophony of noise, change and distraction.

It is critical to be 'selfish,' to make time to sit back, to walk and move at a human pace, and to have a dialogue with ourselves. Whatever our sense of the divine is, this process of renewal is incredibly powerful, and allows us to keep leading.

**◆ FIVE GOOD
RESOURCES**

1. *Man's Search for Meaning*, by Viktor E. Frankl (Beacon Press, 2000).
2. *The Alchemist: A Fable about Following Your Dream*, by Paulo Coelho (HarperCollins, 2006).
3. *The Pilgrimage: A Contemporary Quest for Ancient Wisdom*, by Paulo Coelho (HarperCollins, 2000).
4. *My Camino*, by Sue Kenney (White Knight Publications, 2004).
5. *Desperado*, by The Eagles (CD; Asylum Records, 1973).

In 2010 **ROCCO ROSSI** ran for mayor of the City of Toronto. Though unsuccessful, after a third walk along the Camino following the election, Rocco decided to run for MPP in the upcoming provincial election in October 2011. Rocco has a breadth of experience working in the private and non-profit sectors. Prior to becoming the CEO of the Heart & Stroke Foundation of Ontario he was president and COO, MGI Software; VP, Interactive Media, Labatt/ Interbrew; and VP, Strategic Planning and New Media, The Toronto Star. Rocco has served on both private-sector and non-profit boards, and has volunteer affiliations with several community organizations, including the United Way of Greater Toronto, the Ivey Foundation, New Haven Learning Centre and the Empire Club of Canada.

◔ INSTITUTIONAL CHANGE

Alok Mukherjee

1 Know yourself; know the lay of the land

2 Lay the groundwork fast, and don't settle for a half loaf; build support, and find allies within and without

3 If you can, find a new management team, let it be your ambassador, and resolve differences constructively

4 Use power strategically and with compassion

5 Assess, evaluate and communicate on an ongoing basis

WE ALL KNOW the expression: 'I ain't got all day!' My theme is time: the time it takes to bring about institutional change, the time we have to make such change, and the price we pay if we run out of time before accomplishing real change in the organizations we are involved with.

Like most of you, I joined a board – in my case, the Toronto Police Services Board – because I considered the institution important, and I had a vision for it. My vision for the TPSB centred on making it a much more inclusive organization: in the way it sees itself, serves the community, makes decisions, sets priorities, uses public money, acts as a large employer and responds to the needs and expectations of the residents of Toronto. These aren't just far-off goals; I would like to ensure that they have been achieved, or at least that a solid foundation for them has been laid, before my time on the board is up.

Although we're all familiar with the 'ain't got all day' refrain, most of us have also been counselled, at one time or another, that institutional change takes time. (Alternate formulations: 'Be realistic'; 'Don't rock the boat'; 'Don't go too far, or too fast.') The notion that change takes time is perhaps one of the greatest sources of conflict and mistrust between organizations and seekers of change who feel, often rightly, that they have already waited long enough.

I suspect that most organizational change theories have not dealt with the question of time as I have posed it because they have been developed from organizational perspectives, with the aim of making change palatable to those already in power. And from this perspective, the inclination to preserve the status quo can trump the need for change, and certainly the need to move change forward more quickly. My ideas on this subject are therefore not derived from books or theory; they come from praxis.

1 Know yourself; know the lay of the land

It is a great ego boost to be invited to sit on or chair the board of an organization. There is, understandably, an inclination to say yes and a sense of obligation to help an organization in need with your particular expertise, skills, experiences and networks.

But it is extremely important to be clear about your motivation for taking a place on a board, to know what role you want to play as part of the leadership of the organization, and to consider whether you are the right fit for it, and whether it is the right fit for you. Whether you can make a contribution depends not just on what you bring to the table, but equally on whether the organization is ready for you and the ideas – including ones about institutional change – that are part of your vision. This will help ensure you avoid being an ornament, a token – instead of a real agent of change – on any board on which you sit.

In getting to know an organization you might join, pay attention to its informal as well as its formal culture. If you stop with the formal culture, you may well find that while it makes bold pronouncements on matters that may be dear to you, informally it conducts its day-to-day business otherwise. This informal culture is often more powerful than the formal one.

This is an idea that concerns what happens *before* you get involved with an organization, a guard against setting yourself up for failure, frustration or a loss of credibility in the public eye.

2 Lay the groundwork fast, and don't settle for a half loaf build support, and find allies within and without

My second idea is a cluster rather than just an idea; this is because the elements are interdependent.

With the benefit of knowing the lay of the land already, when you take a leadership role on an organization's board, you come equipped with a developed sense of the changes you would like to make.

Organization theory specialists, often working in the abstract, tend to lay out elaborate models of the change process. While they offer valuable insights that should not be disregarded, I have great trouble with their linear, step-by-step approaches. These are based on the assumption that organizations are rational, logical entities and change can be managed by following a blueprint, much like building a house or assembling furniture. The reality is that most organizations deal with a hundred challenges at once. As well, a linear change process that insists that you must take one well-considered step after another requires an extended time frame and – as we already know – we ain't got all day! Nor do those who have waited a long time for change to happen.

When we are urged to be realistic, it is often just another way of asking us to be timid.

This is why I prefer the approach of someone like a web developer, who knows that since the internet is dynamic and constantly evolving, speed rather than perfection is of the essence. The best strategy is to pursue initiative, and then make the corrections and adjustments that may become necessary along the way. This is what I mean by laying the groundwork fast.

In doing so, it is also important not to settle for a half loaf.

This is the opposite of the admonition to be realistic. In seeking institutional change within the finite time we have at our disposal, there is little room for timidity – and when we are urged to be realistic, it is often just another way of asking us to be timid. It is important not only to start fast, but also to be ambitious.

While I advocate starting fast and going far, I do not mean to suggest that you should act without a game plan: it is extremely important to have one. But the plan should not become its own justification, without the flexibility to change course, make adjustments or take advantage of a serendipitous opportunity. In other words, an ambitious agenda of change requires that there be action on many fronts, and your plan must not restrict you from pursuing them.

When you enact such an agenda, there will be those who will push back, counsel patience, advise caution or question your authority. However, when you demonstrate that your actions are ethical and motivated not by self-interest but by the greater good, you will find there are allies within and without the organization. It is important to pay attention to these allies, and to enlist their support for the change you are seeking.

In building this base of support, there is one final consideration to bear in mind. While you are *in* the organization, you are not *of* the organization. That is to say, the mutually supportive relationship you build should not blind you to the fact that your relationship to the organization is not the same as that of management and employees. There are bound to be different interests, but these need not be antagonistic. The supportive relationship, in other words, should be characterized by a creative tension.

3 If you can, find a new management team, let it be your ambassador, and resolve differences constructively

Implementing change is the domain of management rather than boards, and so a board's best plans can prove ineffective, or not be implemented in a timely manner, because of resistance, inertia, incompetence or outright hostility on the part of management. Management, particularly the chief executive of an organization, needs to have the trust and confidence of the board, and to be on the same wavelength regarding the change process. Work to build an alignment between your new direction and your organization's management, but you should not allow so much time that frustration or conflict sets in. If it becomes evident that management is not on board with your changes, you will need to bring in new leadership.

There is, of course, more to it than just changing the management. The quality of the relationship between board and management is equally important. My point is not that the management should be a lackey of the board – the relationship must be between equals. This means you will be challenged by your operational head. Such challenges must be welcomed, because the dialogue that results will lead to balanced decisions that can be effectively implemented.

Implicit in this process is the real possibility that there will be conflict. Conflict is likely because the interests of the board and the operational head are not necessarily identical, though the goals they pursue must be. But conflict is not a negative phenomenon: it can result in great creativity, provided there is an effective process to resolve differences and the disputes are not personalized.

Management is the linchpin; without effective managers, change cannot happen. With honesty, productive tension, mutual respect and understanding of each other's interests, the chances of a change process succeeding are increased significantly.

4 Use power strategically and with compassion

Because change is a process marked by possibilities of conflict, resistance, sabotage, hostility and so on, it is inevitable that the process will involve transactions in power.

Power is not a simple element – it comes in many forms, such as knowledge and expertise power, charisma power, network power and status power. To manage change effectively you must discern which forms of power you possess yourself within the context of your organization, and how best to use them. (Status power, for instance, has limited uses, and should be used only as a last resort.) Power is most effectively wielded when it is the right type for a given set of circumstances.

Above all, the thoughtless use of power can be hurtful, negatively affecting your organization. It is most important to use power wisely and with compassion.

5 Assess, evaluate and communicate on an ongoing basis

You must evaluate the results you achieve with any change process, and do so continually. This helps ensure you don't become complacent, and that you make necessary adjustments and corrections rapidly.

I am not referring to a formal and time-consuming activity but something simpler and more basic, akin to taking a pulse. We need to do this as a matter of course, as part of our routine interactions with people both inside and outside our organization.

Pulse-taking depends on communicating widely and on an ongoing basis, especially with the community your organization serves. Those whom you consider your base of support, those who have advocated for change, need to know that you are pursuing it, and that your efforts are yielding results. At the same time, you need to find out from your community if they are feeling the effects of that change: it is through this process of communication that you'll know if you are being effective.

FIVE GOOD
RESOURCES

1. *Education for Critical Consciousness*, by Paulo Freire (Continuum, 1981), is a classic work of theory based on praxis.

2. *The Web of Inclusion: A New Architecture for Building Great Organizations*, by Sally Helgesen (Doubleday, 1995), offers several models of successful organizational change.

3. *The Multicultural Leader: Life Stories of Influence and Achievement* by Soosan Daghighi Latham (Backalong Books, 2010).

4. *Race to Equity: Disrupting Educational Inequality*, by Tim McCaskell (Between the Lines, 2005), like *The Multicultural Leader*, provides interesting accounts of the work, underlying values and personal histories of some Canadian change agents.

5. *The Careless Society: Community and Its Counterfeits*, by John McKnight (Basic Books, 1995), combines storytelling, political philosophy and an activist's passion for talking about the ability of communities to heal from within.

DR. ALOK MUKHERJEE is the first South Asian to be elected chair of the Toronto Police Services Board. Alok has taught courses on Indian and South Asian culture and society at York University, is managing associate of an Ottawa-based consulting firm, and has many publications in a variety of areas including diversity, inclusivity and anti-racist education. He has held several public appointments including vice-chair and acting chief commissioner of the Ontario Human Rights Commission, has sat on many boards, and has received the Ontario Volunteer Service Award as well as a commendation from the mayor of Toronto.

 # INFLUENCING CHANGE

John Oesch

1 Highlight potential losses

2 Be explicit about 'what's in it for me'

3 Minimize the bias toward the status quo

4 Remember that a pull can be more powerful than a push

5 Ask for a leap of faith

CHANGE IS ONE of the most discussed, yet least understood, aspects of leadership. Though change is a constant in many corporate, government and non-profit organizations, managing change is something we are just not very good at And organizations' leadership can have a very different understanding of the needs and prospects for change than do their staff and volunteers. This is often compounded by a plethora of advice from the 'change management industry,' and confusion about how to proceed reigns.

We do have empirical information about how staff and volunteers experience change; focusing on this can help you sort through the challenge of handling change effectively. Here are some tips on how to successfully influence and manage organizational change:

1 Highlight potential losses

When we talk about change, we may like the sense of hope it creates. For many, however, change can also mean fear of something new and the loss of certainty; that is why there is often so much resistance to change. We know from social psychology that human beings respond much more strongly to loss than to potential benefit. We experience loss more deeply than we experience a comparable gain.

Instead of only preaching the benefits of a change, frame the *absence* of change as a loss: 'We will lose the chance to be more efficient' or 'We will miss out on serving more of our clients.' Stress the opportunity costs.

2 Be explicit about 'what's in it for me'

Change can arouse suspicion and skepticism. It's common for staff to wonder, 'Why does John *really* want us to change the way we deliver our services? Why does he care?' Tackle this suspicion head-on.

Trust your staff, and share with them all the benefits you anticipate from a change you are leading, including any you might derive yourself (increased efficiency, stronger positioning, etc.). If you engage them in the process, they will be more committed to making change work.

3 Minimize the bias toward the status quo

We are all bundles of biases. One of the biggest: a bias in favour of the status quo, which is associated with certainty, familiarity, predictability. Change, by contrast, is associated with uncertainty, and uncertainty creates anxiety.

The best we can do when making decisions is to reduce the effects of our biases. How do you get around the status quo bias? Here's one approach: come up with a set of alternatives to the status quo, and if two or more of them are preferable (which they always will be), remove status quo from your list of courses of action. Undercut the bias by shifting focus: not status quo versus something new, but one potential change versus another.

4 Remember that a pull can be more powerful than a push

When leading change we tend to seek help from consultants, experts on our boards and other mentors – people who have done it before. One place we often fail to look for assistance is among our community members: those who benefit from our services, buy our products or donate to us. These are people who can inspire staff to follow through on change, who can attract change by the force of their enthusiasm.

A donor, for instance, can help 'pull' your organization to change by asking about new service-delivery models and expressing excitement around their implementation. She could say, 'Let me know when you're close to completion and I'll come back with a cheque to help you finish the project.' Your staff will realize it isn't just their boss (i.e., you) telling them to implement a change: people from outside the organization are paying attention and want to see the change happen too.

5 Ask for a leap of faith

We feel most comfortable when we can draw on models, paradigms and data to support a decision. We prefer to draw up business cases and chart out projected revenues – we rely on evidence. We also demand this of our staff, training them to rely on clear evidence and data when making decisions.

You don't have that evidence when embarking on a major organizational change. But don't gloss over this challenge – embrace it. Be honest. Tell your staff that the environment has changed, the economy has changed, the government isn't providing funds any longer. Say simply: 'We're going to change and this is what the change is going to look like. It's over on the other side of this huge crevasse, and I would like you to jump with me.' Capture their imaginations.

FIVE GOOD RESOURCES

1. *12 Angry Men*, directed by Sidney Lumet (movie, 1957).
2. *Influence: The Psychology of Persuasion*, by Robert B. Cialdini (HarperCollins, 2007).
3. *Who Says Elephants Can't Dance? Inside IBM's Historic Turnaround*, by Louis V. Gerstner Jr. (CollinsBusiness, 2002).
4. *Leading Change*, by John P. Kotter (Harvard Business School, 1996).
5. *Difficult Conversations: How to Discuss What Matters Most*, by Douglas Stone et al. (Penguin Books, 2000).

JOHN OESCH *is assistant professor of Organizational Behaviour at the Rotman School of Management. His research interests lie in the areas of decision making, managerial negotiations and organizational justice; his teaching interests are in similar areas and include the role of emotions in management. In 2005 and 2006 he received the Rotman* MBA *and* EMBA *Teaching Awards. John's publication record includes* The Journal of Business Venturing, Social Justice Research, Games and Economic Behavior *and* Organization Science. *He has a PhD from the Kellogg School of Management at Northwestern University, an* MSC *from the University of British Columbia and an* MBA *from the Richard Ivey School of Business, University of Western Ontario.*

STRATEGIC PLANNING

James Appleyard

1 Identify what your organization can do best

2 Align the existing core values within your organization to targeted social needs and priorities

3 Measure performance and strive for improvement in outcomes – identify one crucial measure of success and track it

4 Good strategic planning is about choosing between competing priorities

5 Ensure internal consistency to deliver better outcomes

WHILE STRATEGIC PLANNING is useful, it is *not* essential to every non-profit. New organizations, organizations with charismatic founder-leaders or organizations that are simply too successful to slow down and plan can all survive with unarticulated strategies that allow them to respond to emerging issues and opportunities. Strategic planning also has opportunity costs for which you need to account: valuable energy, time and resources that would otherwise be of use elsewhere are expended in the development of a strategic plan. And even a good strategic plan can end up in a desk drawer collecting dust if it isn't accompanied by an effective plan for implementation.

In short, strategic plans should not be drawn up without careful consideration, or out of a misplaced sense that they are obligatory.

If your organization is ready for a strategic planning exercise, you must first consider who should participate in the process.

In general, a broader consultation is better than an exercise done more exclusively (for example, only by the board of directors or top management). But there is a trade-off if you involve everyone in your organization rather than selecting key members of the leadership team: inclusiveness is resource-intensive and can create unrealistic expectations that turn to disappointment if not all participants' views are represented in the final strategic plan. That said, the sense of community engagement that emerges from a broad consultation is invaluable, and usually outweighs the short-term investment of time and energy.

The key question: how can you make strategic planning most effective?

☛ **The most common reasons organizations engage in strategic planning:**

▶ **Funders ask for strategic plans** as a condition of issuing or maintaining a grant. The hope is that a strategic plan ensures that an organization has a strong sense of direction, and the capacity to absorb the funding being made available.

▶ **A strategic plan is used as a solution to a crisis** arising from a loss of direction or changes in the external environment. (When a crisis results from funding or staffing issues, other tools may be more appropriate.)

▶ **The calendar says, 'It's time.'** If conditions inside or outside the organization have changed substantially since its inception, or since the last strategic plan was developed, a fresh round of strategic planning may be helpful. This kind of strategic planning is most effective when it is born of real need rather than adherence to a predetermined schedule.

1 Identify what your organization can do best

No organization can do everything well. As activities and projects are created over time, an organization may risk losing perspective on the crucial matter of what it can deliver best. Organizations are similar to individuals: we cannot reach our goals if we take on too much. Discover what is most needed in your service/practice area, and determine which of these needs you are best placed to meet. Focus maximum effort on these activities. For multi-service organizations, try to identify a common thread between your activities, and concentrate on those that are the best fit – for the organization, and with each other.

In some cases, it may be judicious to discontinue less important activities entirely. For others, outsourcing or seeking partnerships with other organizations may be good solutions.

2 Align the existing core values within your organization to targeted social needs and priorities

Passion and values drive all successful organizations, but none are more driven by these qualities than non-profits. Staff, directors and volunteers of non-profit organizations often feel they have a calling; however, this passion can run up against the difficult realities of day-to-day management, resource constraints and continually growing needs in the environment. In addition, the depth and breadth of the passions in an organization can inspire the leadership team to try to pursue too many of them at once.

The strategic-planning challenge is to clearly articulate the strongest passions of an organization's leadership – to tap into what already motivates the leadership – and focus activities around these passions, building the organization around them. An exploration of these motivations, and a refinement of your focus, requires an honest and open conversation, which may in turn require a skilled outside facilitator to help animate such discussions.

3 Measure performance and strive for improvement in outcomes – identify one crucial measure of success and track it

While quantitative and financial measures of success are most often found in the corporate sector, they can also be identified in non-profits. As more and more funders look for some way to assess performance, it is important for non-profit organizations to develop *one* critical measure of organizational success and track it carefully. This might be the number of children receiving a healthy meal each day if you're a social service organization, for instance, or the volume of carbon-emission reductions achieved by an environmental non-profit. Choose a measurement of outcomes that closely links your mission to the available resources, and incorporate it (along with other tools) into your program evaluation.

Limiting yourself to one performance measure is a signal that you've decided what is most important for your non-profit, and that you're instilling that value in a disciplined way throughout the organization. It also helps you avoid one trap of using multiple measures: drawing valuable staff time and resources away from program delivery to measure a host of different things.

Can the measure you choose ever be changed? Yes, it is inevitable – and also desirable – that you will refine and adjust the measurements you use as your organization gains more understanding of which performance measures matter most.

Strategic planning is in part the process of clarifying your organization's objectives, but it is also a matter of establishing how you can reach these objectives, and how you'll know when you've started to do so.

4 Good strategic planning is about choosing between competing priorities

Too often, organizations create a strategic plan by simply restating what they are already doing, without taking time to consider why. This is poor strategic planning, and it comes with a high cost.

Even well-positioned organizations must continuously work toward achieving the right balance across their programs and activities: an organization that is focused on children's services may work on both advocacy and service delivery, for instance. A strategic planning exercise offers the opportunity to consider the trade-offs between your organization's various activities, in part based on the passions of the leadership group, as well as signals from the external environment.

5 Ensure internal consistency to deliver better outcomes

Strategic planning requires that you identify four elements that are key to your organization's success: what you can do best (your capacities); what you care about most (your passions and values); how you know it's working (your performance measure); and your future priorities. Once you've made determinations in each category, the strategic-planning process is substantially about identifying and resolving any inconsistencies between these four elements.

A final note. Your strategic plan needs to be practical and flexible. As you engage in the strategic-planning process, ask yourself whether you have the resources and staff to implement the plan you're considering.

Do you have contingency plans to cope with changes in your environment? Can the strategic plan be adapted to accommodate new situations and circumstances – in other words, did you build in the right degree of flexibility for a fast-changing world?

By keeping these questions in mind, and formulating a strategic plan that does the best job possible answering them, you will ensure not only that your plan reflects your organization's values and your community's needs, but that it can actually be implemented.

⮞ FIVE GOOD RESOURCES

1. *Good to Great: Why Some Companies Make the Leap ... and Others Don't,* by Jim Collins (HarperBusiness, 2001).
2. *The Strategy Process: Concepts, Contexts and Cases,* by Henry Mintzberg and James Brian Quinn (Prentice Hall, 1992).
3. *Jack Trout on Strategy,* by Jack Trout (McGraw-Hill, 2004).
4. *The Future of Nonprofits: Innovate and Thrive in the Digital Age,* by David J. Neff & Randal C. Moss (John Wiley and Sons, 2011).
5. *Mastering the Rockefeller Habits: What You Must Do to Increase the Value of Your Growing Firm,* by Verne Harnish (Select Books, 2006).

JAMES APPLEYARD *is* CEO *and chair of Artez Interactive Inc., a provider of web-based 'friendship-powered fundraising' solutions to not-for-profits in North America, Europe and the Pacific, including the Hospital for Sick Children, Free The Children, Salvation Army Canada, Canadian Red Cross, David Suzuki Foundation and World Wildlife Fund. He has also taught management at the undergraduate and graduate levels at the University of Toronto, and has served on various non-profit boards, including the Canadian Merit Scholarship Foundation.*

TURNING YOUR ORGANIZATION AROUND

Paul Davidson

1 Foster a climate of urgency and demonstrate change is possible

2 Be transparent

3 Be tenacious

4 Be humble

5 Promote hope, not fear

I NEVER SET out to become a 'turn-around artist,' and I have never taken a course on organizational change. But the issues that have interested me have led me to positions of leadership in organizations that have required significant transformation in order to remain vital and relevant. Each organization has been in a different sector, and yet the lessons are remarkably similar. Here then are five good ideas about turning your organization around.

1 Foster a climate of urgency and demonstrate change is possible

Change processes often take so long that people lose confidence in them. However, if your organization needs to change, everyone must see and feel that change is happening, not just dismiss it as a consultation exercise or organizational chatter.

Some will claim that you should create a climate of urgency. I reject this. Artificially creating urgency will lead to cynicism. But you do need to *foster* a climate of urgency. When I worked for a CEO of a major Canadian retailer, he reminded me that he had to report results every 90 days. In such markets, 18 months is an eternity. In the social-mission sector we don't usually report to shareholders, but board members and staff alike are often on term contracts – we can't afford to dither, either.

Achieving and celebrating early wins is also critical – this creates momentum for bigger wins downstream. Sometimes the early wins are exceedingly modest and you feel like a lonely cheerleader, but over time they create a climate where people see that change is possible, and that they are contributing to it.

2 Be transparent

Be candid throughout any change process, and put an emphasis on communicating with staff, board members and stakeholders.

Although staff members are often closest to the problem, they can be the last to see the need for change. And when change does seem imminent, they are likely to fear the unknown. Honesty about the need for change, and the form it will take, will ensure that they feel more in control of their own roles within the organization.

Board members *must* know the hard truth about the challenges your organization is facing, your chances for long-term success, and the risks involved in the change process. There can be no surprises.

Dealing with stakeholders can be more difficult. With donors, there is a tendency to withhold all but essential information and to always put on a brave face. Yet a candid discussion that outlines an understanding of the problem and a path forward will earn trust and confidence. Alumni or 'organizational elders' are often more likely to cling to the past; they may be less aware of changes in the external environment that impact your organization. With this group there is a need to affirm that the planned changes are designed to fulfill your organization's central vision.

A candid discussion that outlines an understanding of the problem and a path forward will earn trust and confidence.

3 Be tenacious

A colleague once remarked that the irony of working in social-change organizations is that we are often the most resistant to change ourselves. People are naturally defensive. When asking them to change in any context, there is an implicit criticism that what's currently being done is not good enough. That is why celebrating the early wins is so important. As well, the support of your board is key to persevering through these choppy waters. The best advice I have received is to constantly honour the work and decisions of the past, but insist that new approaches are required to achieve the founders' vision. Be ready for pushback. You may adjust course, but the best advice is to keep moving.

4 Be humble

All of us in this field are part of a very long tradition of working toward greater participation, inclusion and equality in society. Embracing that tradition – remembering that others have gone before, that our predecessors have already made progress and that our contemporaries are doing excellent work – strengthens the likelihood of success.

Learn from one another and from those in other sectors. The success I have had in introducing change has not come from a top-down position of absolute certainty but from engaging people, inviting their participation, honouring their contribution and showing results.

There is an emphasis on so-called 'strong leadership' these days, but durable change requires drawing on the talents and energy of your whole community, not simply imposing a vision on them.

5 Promote hope, not fear

Too often, organizations prey on fears when introducing change. It's the 'if we don't do this, we'll have to shut down' mentality. Moreover, the very nature of our work means it is never finished. Frustration and despair are often our default positions.

Instilling hope – constantly reminding staff, board and stakeholders that the changes you are making will increase your organization's impact – will enable people to adopt or embrace the change, or at least suspend their concerns while you move forward.

To conclude: hope, humilty, tenacity, transparency and urgency are five common approaches to the turnarounds I have had the privilege of leading.

FIVE GOOD
RESOURCES

1. 'The Mary Ellen Carter,' on *Between the Breaks . . . Live!*, by Stan Rogers (CD; Fogarty's Cove Music, 1979). For its sheer grit and determination.

2. 'My Final Hour,' by Margaret Laurence, in *Canadian Literature*, No. 100, Spring 1984. An essay notable for its passion, urgency and integrity.

3. 'New Year's Day Address on Assuming the Presidency,' by Václav Havel, in *Lend Me Your Ears: Great Speeches in History* (edited by William Safire; W. W. Norton & Co., 1992). A remarkable speech.

4. *The Cult of Efficiency*, by Janice Gross Stein (House of Anansi, 2002).

5. *Getting to Maybe: How the World Is Changed*, by Frances Westley, Brenda Zimmerman and Michael Quinn Patton (Random House, 2007).

PAUL DAVIDSON, *president of the Association of Universities and Colleges of Canada since 2009, has played leadership roles in the public, private and voluntary sectors. He was executive director of World University Service of Canada from 2002 to 2009; WUSC is now active on over 70 campuses across Canada and in over 17 countries. Previously, Paul spent seven years in the Canadian book-publishing industry, including five years as executive director of the Association of Canadian Publishers. He also served from 1998 to 2004 as a volunteer on the board of the ALS Society of Canada. In the early 1990s, Paul led the Toronto office of a government relations firm following three years as a political advisor to Ontario's Treasurer. He holds an MA from Queen's University and a BA from Trent University.*

INNOVATION

Suzanne Gibson

1 Think of your cause as
a movement

2 Pump up your entrepreneurial
muscles

3 Seek out and engage
the unusual

4 Create and steward
learning cultures

5 Think to be effective,
not to be right

FOR AN IDEA to take root, it needs a good producer and promoter to inspire, motivate, cajole, alleviate fears, shift perceptions and garner results. And that champion must be courageous, determined and flexible.

1 Think of your cause as a movement

There is a wonderful Ethiopian saying: 'When spiderwebs are woven together, they can catch a lion.' The moral: we can collectively weave networks and strategies that help us overcome the most powerful challenges in our work.

We are each, individuals and organizations, part of a system. When you begin to envision your cause as a movement, who and what else do you see yourself connecting to? Where can you link to others and where do you have points of influence that you can tap into?

2 Pump up your entrepreneurial muscles

Entrepreneurs are characterized by their ability to see opportunities where others don't – but recognizing opportunity is a skill, not an innate character trait. As a non-profit leader, you need to build your entrepreneurial muscles, your capacity to spot exciting new possibilities from which your organization might benefit.

Successful leaders have honed their ability to identify opportunities and transcend the traditional. These leaders are often at the forefront of positive change because they focus on opportunities rather than threats; they are forward-thinking and acutely aware of what they have to work with in their environment. They anticipate situations and identify challenges – always along with strategies to address them.

☛ **How to Boost Your Entrepreneurial Muscles**

▶ **Moniter emerging trends:** Understand the constantly changing subtleties of your environment. Track trends in the media, read voraciously, engage with your networks and learn what others in your community have their eyes on.

▶ **Study best practices:** Looking at what others are doing will both save you time and open your mind to new approaches to your mission and goals.

▶ **Assess risks and take some:** Social innovators are good at gauging risks. They are risk takers, but the risks they take are carefully considered. If a strategy is risky but seems worth exploring, smart innovators create contingency plans and weigh alternative courses of action; they take nothing for granted. Ask yourself what opportunities you can maximize in light of your organization's strengths and weaknesses.

3 Seek out and engage the unusual

Creativity sometimes involves creating something original, but more often it is a matter of combining existing elements in new and unexpected ways.

If you're considering a new venture or project, ask yourself what unusual suspects you can involve in the undertaking. Who are some of the least likely groups to engage with, and what fresh insights might they bring? Who might be the most obvious people to engage with, and who might they know that you hadn't considered involving before? Different perspectives can open up new approaches to your work – this is an investment in your future ability to innovate.

Similarly, ask yourself if there are unusual ways you can combine different strategies or methodologies to help achieve your goals. This can range from collaborating with unexpected partners to deliver services, to promoting your programs in unexpected media or locations. Unusual communications and messaging strategies can build momentum for your cause, and unexpected partnerships can expose your organization to new audiences.

4 Create and steward learning cultures

A healthy organization is a learning organization: one that is committed to continual improvement, one in which staff are exposed to new approaches and new ways of thinking.

The strongest leaders have an unquenchable curiosity about the world – they never believe that what they know is enough. They ask everyone around them for fresh insights. They weave ideas together from a variety of sources, never believing that they alone have the right answer.

If you're considering a new venture or project, ask yourself what unusual suspects you can involve in the undertaking.

Innovators build their organizations' culture of innovation. Encourage people in your organization to think productively. Ask them how many different ways they can look at a problem. How can they rethink it? Reward experimentation and challenge your peers and staff members not to take anything for granted.

5 Think to be effective, not to be right

You don't have to be right every time. Being effective means being right only at the end.

Often the best leaders and innovators work hard to protect seedling ideas because one day they will sprout up into something marvellous. We must learn to remove our egos from the thinking process and eliminate our need to solve everything immediately; for a while, just exploring is okay. Embracing uncertainty requires courage, adaptability and a willingness to be wrong.

FIVE GOOD RESOURCES

1. *How to Change the World: Social Entrepreneurs and the Power of New Ideas*, by David Bornstein (Oxford University Press, 2004).
2. *Enterprising Nonprofits: A Toolkit for Social Entrepreneurs*, by J. Gregory Dees, Jed Emerson and Peter Economy (John Wiley & Sons, 2001).
3. *How to Think Like Leonardo da Vinci: Seven Steps to Genius Every Day*, by Michael J. Gelb (Dell, 1998).
4. *The Tipping Point: How Little Things Can Make a Big Difference*, by Malcolm Gladwell (Back Bay Books, 2002).
5. *Stanford Social Innovation Review*, Quarterly Journal (Center for Social Innovation, Stanford Graduate School of Business).

A non-profit management consultant, **SUZANNE GIBSON** supports new and established organizations as they go through the process of 'dreaming big' and uniting around a strategy to turn those dreams into reality. As founding executive director of Raising the Roof, Canada's first national charity dedicated to alleviating homelessness, Suzanne discovered that people, resources and money follow innovative ideas. Since then, she has committed herself to exploring social entrepreneurship, creativity, invention and social innovation. In addition to consulting, Suzanne also enjoys her work as an instructor for a variety of institutions, including York University's Schulich School for Business. She has taken a leadership role on six provincial and national volunteer boards, and speaks extensively on leadership, social entrepreneurship, governance, fund development and other issues of importance to the nonprofit sector.

2

ORGANIZATIONAL EFFECTIVENESS

RISK IS an essential element of any change process; without risk it is difficult to foster a climate of organizational innovation, and impossible to address any systemic issues that you might be facing.

– Derek Ballantyne

LEADING AN INCLUSIVE ORGANIZATION

Kay Blair

1 Think of leadership as an action, not a position

2 Invest in the talent in your organization

3 Support and encourage self-directed teams within your organization

4 Make inclusiveness part of your organization's DNA

5 Embrace diversity

PEOPLE CANNOT BE inspired by charts, data, memos, mission statements, measurements, systems and processes alone. These tools are important for improving performance, but it's organizations that are inclusive that have the greatest capacity to unleash human potential, and that allow individual and collective creativity to flourish.

Inclusive leadership is the ability to step back to engage and empower others in your organization. This requires a true commitment to involving *all* your organization's talent in decision making. Consistently practicing a culture of inclusiveness – through teamwork, sharing, learning and providing opportunities for growth – will create real commitment among your staff.

1 Think of leadership as an action, not a position

Leadership as action is about engaging individuals and teams to make decisions – establishing an environment in which decision making is participatory rather than hierarchical.

Staff should feel secure in their workplace: they need a sense of belonging, community and connectedness. Allowing them to participate in decision processes, providing opportunities for them to express their opinions and contribute their perspectives, all help to foster a sense of inclusion, which contributes to a sense of security. This is especially true during a process of change. Because change requires that we give up the familiar it can disrupt staff's feeling that they are an important part of a coherent and stable whole. In an inclusive organization, decision and change processes are not top-down, they are participatory.

A truly inclusive organization is collaborative rather than hierarchical, and one in which processes are not standardized. Organizations that are organically structured allow for engagement and inclusion.

2 Invest in the talent in your organization

An inclusive organization develops the skills of its staff, and allows them to advance via transparent promotional practices. Create chances for staff to take on new tasks and responsibilities, and provide coaching and mentoring to help them meet new challenges. Leadership training within your organization must be transparent and understood: make sure the criteria for selecting staff for advancement, training and rewards are clear.

3 Support and encourage self-directed teams within your organization

A team approach ensures that leadership is distributed in your organization; this creates an empowered workplace. It reinforces the principles of inclusion as workers come to understand that, like managers, they too have a say in an organization's output.

A self-directed, high-performing team draws on the skills, knowledge, and talents of all team members. And an organization with such a team will be one in which staff hold themselves accountable for optimal performance, and develop mutual trust and respect. Successes are shared, and failures provide valuable learning experiences for the whole team.

4 Make inclusiveness part of your organization's DNA

An organization's DNA refers to its unique processes and qualities, the elements that cannot be easily replicated. It is what creates value for an organization and determines how it will function. Critical elements of an organization's DNA include the flow of information and access to communication tools and processes; staff engagement and motivational tools; and the decision-making models employed throughout the organization. An organization that has inclusiveness built into its DNA is one in which everyone on staff realizes that decisions are not restricted to the senior leadership, and allows for everyone at all levels to engage creatively in its development and growth.

5 Embrace diversity

One essential aspect of inclusivity is ensuring that your organization is diverse, and that diversity goals are reflected in your core organizational strategies (strategic plan, human-resources policies and so on). This is part of what it means to value what individuals bring to the workplace and to maintain a workplace that is genuinely accepting.

FIVE GOOD RESOURCES

1. *Ethics, the Heart of Leadership*, edited by Joanne B. Ciulla (Praeger, 1998).
2. *The Seven Habits of Highly Effective People: Powerful Lessons in Personal Change*, by Steven R. Covey (Free Press, 2004).
3. *Leadership Is an Art*, by Max DePree (Doubleday, 2004).
4. *Leading Change: The Argument for Values-Based Leadership*, by James O'Toole (Ballantine Books, 1996).
5. *Leadership and the New Science: Discovering Order in a Chaotic World*, by Margaret J. Wheatley (Berrett-Koehler, 2001).

KAY BLAIR *has been executive director of Community MicroSkills Development Centre, a community agency serving immigrants, low-income women and youth since 1988. She is chair of the William Osler Health System and has served two terms as president of Ontario Council of Agencies Serving Immigrants. Kay frequently serves as a consultant to government and community groups on issues of access, equity and organizational and community development. Among her awards are Canada's Most Powerful Women: Top 100 Award – Trailblazer (2004); the YWCA Woman of Distinction – Community Leadership (2006); the Premier's Award – Community and Social Services (2007); and the Outstanding Achievement Award (2011) from Jamaica Canadian Association. Kay holds an MBA with a specialization in Leadership from Royal Roads University.*

📁 SHARED SERVICES

Sharon B. Cohen

1 Consider shared services as a strategy for capacity building

2 Start with early wins

3 Manage your shared services implementation like a project

4 Leverage modern service-delivery strategies

5 Get the governance right

SHARING SERVICES SIMPLY means joining forces with other departments or organizations to make your organization stronger, more efficient and more effective.

A bit more technically: a shared services model is one that supports the consolidation of certain business functions on the basis of an enterprise (e.g., organizational), a sector (e.g., children's aid societies) or a community (e.g., geographic), and the transfer of these business functions into specialist centres under shared management. These shared functions are then operated as freestanding 'businesses' accountable to their clients – namely all the participating departments or organizations. Such services might include contact centres, financial processing and accounting, payroll and benefits, legal and other professional services (such as labour relations advice), facilities management, insurance and risk management, and information technology.

A shared services model can offer many benefits. It can help you drive down costs (organizations often report savings of 10 to 40 percent); allow you to redeploy savings to mission-critical areas; create opportunities for maximizing scarce resources; eliminate redundancy and duplication; and enable you to increase the quality of the services you provide.

A shared services model attempts to strike a balance between benefits that can typically be achieved through a highly centralized service-delivery model, which is very efficient but not always responsive to individual needs or idiosyncratic cases, and the benefits of what might be called a distributed model, where every organization independently provides all its own business functions.

Shared services are usually adopted as part of a strategy for modernization, transformation and capacity building. To realize the benefits, there must be sustained commitment to the shared services model, at least for a few years, while investments are made in people, processes and systems.

For most governments and larger organizations, the earliest benefits are typically seen at the transactional level: for example, multiple financial, payroll and IT systems can be pulled together, redesigned and streamlined. In non-profit organizations, early wins can be achieved in program delivery. Welcome services, facilities management, procurement and training are good candidates for a shared services model, as are back-office functions such as human resources and information technology support.

1 Consider shared services as a strategy for capacity building

Have clear and unambiguous goals that integrate shared services within a broader vision for your organization or sector. Seek respected and trusted leadership from within your sector to articulate and lead the change.

2 Start with early wins

Engage your sector's leadership and stakeholders in identifying the ideal project scope; work together to determine which services are most amenable to shared services solutions.

3 Manage your shared services implementation like a project

Articulate your 'from/to' story and prepare an action plan to bridge the gap between where you are and where you want to be. Have a clear sense of the baseline position from which you are starting, and identify measurable financial and non-financial benefits of moving to shared services. Prepare the business case and implementation plan.

4 Leverage modern service-delivery strategies

Contact centres, service agreements, portal technology and sector best practices can all help you modernize your operations and make you more efficient in your work. The investments in your shared services journey will be transformational!

5 Get the governance right

Be thoughtful about defining your sector and choosing your partners. Effective governance will ensure that investments are made, milestones are met, and wins are realized. Define the rules of engagement and make sure the distribution of responsibilities is clear. Have a shared understanding of goals and outcomes.

FIVE GOOD RESOURCES

1. *Implementing Shared Services in the Public Sector: The Pillars of Success*, by Carolyn Farquhar, Jennifer Fultz and Andrew Graham (The Conference Board of Canada, 2006).

2. *Shared Services: Mining for Corporate Gold*, by Barbara Quinn, Robert Cooke and Andrew Kris (Financial Times/Prentice Hall, 2000).

3. *Shared Services: Adding Value to the Business Units*, by Donniel S. Schulman, John R. Dunleavy, Martin J. Harmer and James S. Lusk (John Wiley & Sons, 1999).

4. Conference Proceedings, Public Sector Shared Services 2006: Transforming Service Delivery (The Conference Board of Canada, November 2006).

5. Conference Proceedings, Public Sector Shared Services: How to Deliver Value for Your Organization (The Conference Board of Canada, November 2005).

SHARON COHEN *is the founding president of Shared Solutions Management Consulting, providing advice and support to the public, broader public and non-profit sectors in shared services design and implementation, agency start-ups and transformations, and business strategy and solutions. Previously, she was the CEO of Ontario Shared Services, at that time one of the world's largest public-sector shared services organizations. She holds an Honours BA in Political Science from York University, and an MA in Political Economy from the University of Toronto.*

⚠ MANAGING RISK

Derek Ballantyne

1 Understand what constitutes
a risk for you and your
organization (or, Try to bite
off only what you can chew)

2 Support risk-taking –
really!

3 Pay
attention

4 Don't fall for your
own story

5 Celebrate success and learn
from failure

RISK IS AN essential ingredient of change. Risk is often perceived as negative, as its origins lie in events, reactions or decisions that are beyond your control. However, risk is also an essential element of any change process; without risk it is difficult to foster a climate of organizational innovation and impossible to address any systemic issues that you might be facing.

We often think of risk as financial, but it is much more than that: there is risk to reputation, risk to organizational mission and risk to personal employment, all of which come along with organizational change.

The concept of managing risk implies that risk can be controlled and its negative impacts mitigated. When innovating – when pursuing courses of action that by definition have risks built in – it is true we can look at what other organizations have done and learn from them; this is one way of mitigating risk. However, each organization will face a unique set of circumstances when making changes; the risks are different each time because of differences in organizational capacity, financial resources, and the people who are charged with making the changes.

At Toronto Community Housing a few years ago, we set out on an agenda of transformation and accepted that risk would be part of that. We knew we had to embrace risk. What we were not as prepared for was just *how* to do that. Here is some of what we learned as we moved ahead with our plans.

1 Understand what constitutes a risk for you and your organization (or, Try to bite off only what you can chew)

It is impossible to identify the full scope of risks ahead of time, but it is possible to identify the risks involved in an undertaking, put these in a context that others can understand and determine how they can be measured. When embarking on a project or change process, force yourself to acknowledge what might not work and why. Here are some important questions to consider:

Do you know the risks you will face? A good friend once told me that all of the problems sitting on his desk started life as good ideas. Taking the time to think through each new idea and understand its risks may help you understand what can go wrong and how to prevent it.

It's easy to assess financial risk, and more difficult but equally important to assess whether there is organizational resilience should a project fail.

Can you afford to invest in an initiative and not succeed? Will this jeopardize your ability to deliver programs and services? This is the simple test of whether the costs of failure are more than you can bear. It's easy to assess financial risk, and more difficult but equally important to assess whether there is organizational resilience should a project fail. Boards are particularly hard to read in this respect as they are more sensitive to an organization's reputation and to potential impacts on funders.

Does your board understand the risks you are taking? Your board must fully understand the risks involved in delivering a program. It's often tempting to paint a glossy picture of future outcomes, but this increases the level of risk for organizational leadership when things – inevitably – don't work as planned.

Are you taking risks to deliver on an organizational priority? Anyone in an organization has a limited amount of non-financial 'capital.' If you are the champion of an initiative or the sponsor of something identified as a risk, this capital should be reserved for organizational priorities. If you're going to incur risks, do so for worthwhile goals.

2 Support risk-taking – really!

Embarking on something that has been identified as a risk needs an organization's full support to have the best chance of succeeding. Support starts with leadership: whatever the initiative, it must have the attention of those with the power and authority to keep things on track. This includes the board, the senior management team, and, in some cases, your funding partners.

Support also entails providing sufficient human and financial support to achieve a successful outcome. Launching an initiative with great hope and little practical viability is a risk strategy with minimal rewards.

While putting effort into managing change and its inherent risks, do not take your eye off your organization's daily business.

3 Pay attention

Getting an idea off the ground is simple. Achieving some success requires that you pay sufficient attention to the key initiatives you launch, and make sure that others in your organization do the same.

There is no set formula for this; some prefer rigid project management systems, others less formal reporting. The key is that leadership is exercised throughout the process, and if staff or others are asked to implement an idea, they have the authority and support to do so.

A caution here: while putting effort into managing change and its inherent risks, do not take your eye off your organization's daily business. If your core services fail because of inattention or diverted resources, then the change you're trying to implement will also fail.

It is also important in this process that error and failure are recognized if and as they happen; you need to know if you aren't succeeding, and pulling the plug on a project should always be an option.

4

Don't fall for your own story

Most of us are by nature defensive. When we are deeply invested in a new idea, we often do not hear the voices of dissenters. When you're engaged in something that carries risks for you and your organization, listen carefully to those who disagree. Deliberately seek advice from those who have different points of view. Draw from the experience of others. You want to know when you're headed off the cliff.

As an executive director or senior manager, it will ultimately be your job to decide on a course of action; make sure you are being critical and reflective while making those decisions. Do not always believe your inner voice, or those who depend on the success of an initiative you're considering. Falling for your own story compounds risk and is often a quick path to failure.

5

Celebrate success and learn from failure

This is the most obvious idea, but the one that is most often missed. If you are in an organization that is willing to take risks, then there is an absolute need to recognize your successes. Celebrating these provides essential reinforcement, which encourages further innovation and supports risk-taking as part of your organizational culture. More importantly, it makes sure people learn from failures and provides assurance that failure does not mean pulling back from further risk-taking down the road. A good system of post-mortem analysis and open discussion with those involved, including decision makers such as a board, is important.

**FIVE GOOD
RESOURCES**

1. Best Practices in Risk Management: Private and Public Sectors
   Internationally (Treasury Board of Canada Secretariat, 1999)
   (www.tbs-sct.gc.ca/pubs_pol/dcgpubs/RiskManagement/
   rm-ps1_e.asp).
2. 'Everyday Risk Management,' by Matthew Leitch (2003)
   (http://www.internalcontrolsdesign.co.uk/edrm/index.shtml).
3. *Exposing the Elephants: Creating Exceptional Nonprofits*,
   by Pamela J. Wilcox (John Wiley & Sons, 2006).
4. *Improving Quality and Performance in Your Non-Profit Organization:
   An Introduction to Change Management Strategies for the 21st Century*,
   by Gary M. Grobman (White Hat Communications, 1999).
5. 'Act on Facts, Not Faith,' by Jeffrey Pfeffer and Robert I. Sutton, in
   Stanford Social Innovation Review, Spring 2006
   http://www.ssireview.org/articles/entry/act_on_facts_not_faith/.

DEREK BALLANTYNE *was CEO of the Toronto Community Housing Corporation, the largest social-housing provider in Canada and the second largest
in North America, from 2001 to 2009. He previously served as CEO of the
Toronto Housing Company and prior to that was general manager, City Living, City of Ottawa Non-Profit Housing. Derek has also worked in the sector
in volunteer roles, including that of founding board member of the Ontario
Non-Profit Housing Association and chair of Raising the Roof, a charitable
organization dedicated to finding solutions to homelessness. He currently sits
on the board of Ontario's Social Housing Services Corporation.*

NOT-FOR-PROFIT CORPORATIONS LAW

Sheila Crummey

1 Understand and stick to your mandate

2 Decide whether you need directors' and officers' liability insurance

3 Understand non-profit legislation

4 Be familiar with the Canada Revenue Agency fundraising policy

5 Know the parameters of legitimate political advocacy for your charity

EVERY NOT-FOR-PROFIT ORGANIZATION (also called a non-profit) is governed by corporate law; registered charities are also governed by the Income Tax Act. The following five good ideas are focused on ensuring that your non-profit, especially if it is a charity, is operated in compliance with these various laws. Such compliance is a form of risk management that's important for all directors and officers of non-profit organizations.

1 Understand and stick to your mandate

A non-profit's mandate is set out in its Letters Patent, the document issued by the government by which it is incorporated. Unlike for-profit corporations, non-profits may only do what their Letters Patent permit. If the directors of a non-profit allow the corporation to pursue undertakings outside the authority of the corporation's objects (its legally established scope of activities), this increases the risk of exposure to personal liability for the consequences of those actions. It is therefore important for all directors to review the corporation's Letter Patent and any Supplementary Letters Patent, and ensure that the activities of the corporation are authorized by the objects set out in those documents. When a new program is proposed within your organization, always consider whether it is designed to achieve a stated object in your Letters Patent. (You can always amend the Letters Patent to expand these objects, but if you are a registered charity you'll need approval from the Public Guardian and Trustee, and from the Canada Revenue Agency.)

If you are a charity you must also file an annual Charities Return: this describes programs you are running and the resources you are using to conduct those activities. If a program or activity falls clearly outside the scope of your objects and/or is non-charitable, the CRA could take exception – devoting resources to non-charitable activities is grounds for deregistration. Again, make sure your organization's activities fall within its stated mandate.

2 Decide whether you need directors' and officers' liability insurance

Federal and provincial non-profit legislation permits corporations to provide indemnities to directors and officers. This ensures that directors and officers who suffer a loss or are out of pocket due to actions taken in the course of fulfilling their duties can be reimbursed by their organization. Legislation also allows non-profits to take out directors' and officers' liability insurance.

☞Criteria to consider before giving indemnity or purchasing directors' and officers' insurance:

► degree of risk to which director or officer is or may be exposed
► whether risk can be eliminated or significantly reduced by means other than indemnities or D&O insurance
► whether the amount or cost of insurance is reasonable in relation to risk
► whether cost of insurance is reasonable in relation to revenue
► whether the indemnification or purchase of D&O insurance advances the administration and management of the charitable property

Also, note that:
► a charity cannot pay an indemnity or purchase D&O insurance if, as a result, the amount of debt and liability of the corporation would exceed the value of the charitable property or would render the corporation insolvent
► endowment funds created to provide grants to other registered charities should not attract risk and therefore may not be available to fund indemnities or D&O insurance against other risks.

3 Understand non-profit legislation

Both Ontario and Canada are expected to have new non-profit legislation in place by fall 2012. These new regimes will change financial reporting obligations: notably, the new rules set dollar thresholds for annual revenue that will determine whether the non-profit organization needs an audit or may waive the audit in favour of a review engagement. Review engagement is less onerous (and less expensive) than an audit.

Another change to bear in mind is that under both the federal and Ontario regimes, soliciting corporations and public-benefit corporations will be required to have a minimum of three directors (this is no different than the current regime), but two of the directors cannot be management (this is a change from the current regime). Both the new federal and Ontario legislations also provide enhanced members' rights. To prepare for these new rules, all non-profits should review their membership structure.

Under the new federal legislation, a non-profit must file Articles of Continuance (amend its constating document) in accordance with the new legislation no later than three years after the new legislation is proclaimed in force, and will be subject to dissolution if it fails to do so. Under the Ontario legislation, if a non-profit fails to amend its articles to be in conformity with the new statute within three years of enactment, the statute deems the organizations' articles to be amended to be in conformity. You will therefore want to ensure that you take appropriate action proactively. All non-profits, whether federally incorporated or incorporated in Ontario, should review these new regimes and make plans to comply in the ways that best serve their organization.

4 Be familiar with the Canada Revenue Agency fundraising policy

The CRA publishes guidelines on fundraising; these were developed in response to media and public pressure for fuller disclosure of CRA's internal guidelines on fundraising and out of a concern for accountability from charities about fundraising.

All charities must report their fundraising expenses to the CRA. The relationship between costs and revenues is a large part of what determines the CRA's approach to your organization.

FUNDRAISING RATIOS AND THEIR EFFECTS

Ratio of cost to revenue over a fiscal period	CRA Approach
Under 35%	Unlikely to generate questions or concerns.
35% and above	The CRA will examine the average ratio over recent years to determine if there is a trend of high fundraising costs. The higher the ratio, the more likely it is that the CRA will have concerns and need a more detailed assessment of expenditures.
Above 70%	This level will raise concerns with the CRA. The charity must be able to provide an explanation and rationale for this level of expenditure to show that it is in compliance with CRA guidelines.

What all this means is that your costs must be balanced relative to your revenues. Charities must plan fundraising campaigns carefully. It's essential to make sure you have the appropriate oversight and cost-control measures in place at your organization. Have clear policies laid out regarding matters like procurement, monitor receipts carefully, conduct periodic evaluations of your fundraising activities, conduct internal audits, and use volunteers to the greatest extent possible. Transparency is also a must: CRA's expectation is that there will be complete disclosure of fundraising costs and revenue.

☛**Areas of potential concern:**
- ► sole-source fundraising contracts without proof of fair market value
- ► non-arm's-length fundraising contracts without proof of fair market value
- ► fundraising initiatives or arrangements that are not well documented
- ► activities where most of gross revenues go to contracted non-charitable parties
- ► commission-based fundraiser remuneration
- ► misrepresentations in fundraising solicitations or disclosure about fundraising or financial performance

5 Know the parameters of legitimate political advocacy for your charity

Charities are permitted to engage in political activities, but only if these activities further the charity's goals and the percentage of resources used is within prescribed limits. (Examples of political activities: publishing commentary related to your charity's goals, participating in a march or demonstration, arranging a media campaign.)

LIMITS ON CHARITABLE RESOURCES GOING TO POLITICAL ACTIVITIES	
Charities with revenues of:	Allowable expenditures
Less than $50,000	Up to 20%
$50,000–100,000	Up to 15%
Greater than $200,000	Up to 10%

There are also some political activities that are prohibited for charities, notably direct or indirect support for or opposition to any candidate for office or political party. Examples of this would include endorsing an election candidate in your charity's newsletter, distributing leaflets highlighting a lack of government support for your charity's goals, preparing dinner for campaign organizers of a political party, inviting specific candidates from a jurisdiction to speak at your event but excluding others.

→ FIVE GOOD RESOURCES

1. 'Primer for Directors of Not-for-Profit Corporations: Right, Duties and Practices,' Industry Canada (http://www.ic.gc.ca/eic/site/cilp-pdci.nsf/vwapj/Primer_en.pdf/$FILE/Primer_en.pdf)

2. 'Not-for-Profit Incorporator's Handbook,' Ontario Ministry of Government Services and the Office of the Public Guardian and Trustee for Ontario (http://www.attorneygeneral.jus.gov.on.ca/english/family/pgt/nfpinc/Not_for_Profit_Incorporators_Handbook_en.pdf).

3. Ontario Regulation 4/01 under the Charities Accounting Act; (Ontario), R.S.O. 1190, c.C.10.

4. Articles by Wayne D. Gray of McMillan LLP published in:
   ▶ Corporate Brief, CCH, August 2008, Number 168: 'Bill C-62 (Canada Not-for-profit Corporations Act) Canadian not-for-profit ('NFP') corporate law may soon leap forward 89 years'
   ▶ Corporate Brief, CCH, June 2010, Number 190: 'More Help Coming for Those Who Help Others: Bill 65 (Ontario Not-for-Profit Corporations Act, 2010)'

5. Canada Revenue Agency, Policy Statement, Political Activities, CPS-022, September 2, 2003.

SHEILA CRUMMEY, *a partner with McMillan, has been certified as a specialist in estates and trusts law by the Law Society of Upper Canada. Her years of working as a senior tax manager in a national accounting firm have given her broad experience in tax planning, particularly for business owners. Her charities and not-for-profit practice involves providing advice to individuals on structuring tax-effective philanthropy. She also advises public charitable and not-for-profit organizations, as well as private family foundations, on a range of issues including governance matters, regulatory compliance and risk management. Sheila is a frequent speaker on topics related to estate planning at events sponsored by the Law Society of Upper Canada and the Ontario Bar Association.*

⚠ DEALING WITH A LARGE-SCALE EMERGENCY

Thomas Appleyard

 1 Perform a risk assessment

 2 Facilitate the community's development of robust solutions

 3 Focus on occupational health and safety

 4 Develop your own emergency response plan and partnerships

5 Plan for business continuity

GUIDANCE FOR LARGE organizations who need to deal with large-scale emergencies is widely available. Far less is available for small organizations, especially small community-based organizations that have to respond to large-scale emergencies – such as public health emergencies – because the needs of their clients and communities change as external circumstances do.

With an emphasis on the early response phase during an emergency, these five good ideas are intended to help fill this gap.

1 Perform a risk assessment

Whether you are in the preparedness phase planning for possible future events, or in the response phase figuring out what your organization will do today and tomorrow, performing a risk assessment is essential. This will allow you to reflect on what an emergency might mean for your operations, clients, partners, suppliers and community.

Many tools can be used to structure the risk assessment process. A commonly used one is the HIRA – Hazard Identification and Risk Assessment. With HIRAs, specific hazards that may affect the organization (for example, influenza outbreaks, tornadoes or blackouts) are identified and potential impacts are assessed. Municipalities in Ontario are required to perform HIRAs regularly. You may be able to get a copy of the HIRA for your area. One of the great benefits of conducting your own internal HIRA is that it will help you visualize what your organization could look like as an emergency is under way. This visualization step can be extremely useful for planning.

Employees may wonder as an emergency begins, 'Will I come to work each day and find out what my job is as I arrive, or am I going to do the same job I usually do? Are people still going to sit at their desks or will they be working from home? Will there be screeners at the door asking people about symptoms?' Having the answers to these questions – even if they are just a best guess – is very helpful.

This can't just be a theoretical exercise: actually do a simulation of how your organization would function in emergency circumstances. If, for instance, you are preparing for a large-scale public health emergency, practice the strategies you might use; if needed, have everyone in your office go through the steps of putting on and taking off personal protective equipment, determine exactly where screening stations would be, practice taking someone's temperature – the really practical, skill-based things you'll need to implement in moments of actual emergency. You'll find that it's only when staff can truly visualize the types of scenarios you might face that you can engage in deeper, richer and more collaborative planning for those circumstances.

Compared to merely complicated events, complex events require less emphasis on expert input and more emphasis on multiple perspectives.

A problem with HIRAS, however, is that we are notoriously poor at predicting hazards. Think about the events we didn't see coming (SARS, the 2003 blackout) and the (so far) non-events that we thought were coming (the avian influenza pandemic, Y2K). Often what goes into HIRAS is information about past events. It is important to look at these and identify what was learned, but it's also important to ask how the organization and community have *changed* since those events, and what that might mean for the response required.

While we're pretty bad at predicting hazards, we're better at predicting consequences for our organization and communities. This means we can shift our thinking from specific contingency planning to broader scenario planning. There are common consequences to a whole range of emergencies that small organizations may face: high staff absenteeism; disruption in supply lines; heightened risk of staff illness, injury or death; heightened risk of client illness, injury or death; disruption of IT resources; significant property damage; loss of records; inability of clients to access the interventions established; or even increased threats to health equity caused by these same interventions. Planning can be done based on these categories of effects rather than specific hazards.

2 Facilitate the community's development of robust solutions

One of the factors that will determine whether workers come to work during an emergency is whether they trust the information provided by their employer. Employers can build that trust by talking about employee concerns.

Asking about concerns – an inherent part of the risk assessment process – helps develop organizational trust. This organizational trust actually is a robust solution – by which I mean an effective problem-solving strategy in a large range of scenarios.

When thinking about robust solutions to emergency management problems, more and more literature is stressing the importance of paying attention to the complexity of events. My favourite sentence in the emergency management literature comes from an article by Preeta M. Banerjee and Joseph T. Mahoney regarding the *Columbia* space-shuttle explosion. They described the 'recovery window' as the uncertain period of time after it was realized that something was going seriously wrong. They said: 'In highly uncertain situations ... entertaining hunches, reasoning by analogy, imagining potential scenarios, and experimenting with novel, ill-defined alternatives become essential.'

Compared to merely complicated events, complex events require less emphasis on expert input and more emphasis on multiple perspectives. Engaging stakeholders in activities such as the ones described above not only makes the process more inclusive, it becomes essential emergency management practice. Complex events require attentive sense-making skills and watchfulness.

3 Focus on occupational health and safety

In Ontario, the Occupational Health and Safety Act trumps the Emergency Management and Civil Protection Act. It's impossible to talk about responding to an emergency without talking about occupational health and safety, because occupational health and safety must be your top priority. For health emergencies, this includes paying careful attention to infection prevention and control.

One major strategy for preventing and controlling infection during a community outbreak is handwashing. It is the cornerstone of influenza pandemic response before a vaccine is available, and there is a lot of evidence that we aren't anywhere near as good at hand hygiene as we think we are. One of the reasons people say they don't want to wash their hands frequently is because their skin may get cracked and chapped. Providing hand moisturizer for staff and clients has been shown to increase rates of handwashing. Similarly, it has been great to see hand-sanitizer dispensers stay up after the H1N1 crisis was declared over. In all our organizations, let's make sure we don't lose this momentum.

In many organizations people are still encouraged and given incentive to come to work when they are ill with a cough or fever. (Some recent research says that 84 percent of employees feel pressured to come to work when they are sick.) We need to change the culture surrounding sick leave – if we can't get this right between infectious disease outbreaks, we'll never get it right during one. People who are coming to work when they have a cough and fever are doing far more harm than good. We need to support the idea that it is preferable to stay home while ill through policy and through example from leadership, and by simply telling people to go home.

4 Develop your own emergency response plan and partnerships

It's worth spending time in a planning process to focus exclusively on your daily functions. During this stage, make it against the rules to think about what other organizations will do. No one is allowed to ask: What if the TTC shuts down? What if Loblaws can't access any food at all? What if the shelters shut down? This is the time to work on a plan in your own organization. What are the risks you think you may face? How can you address some of the common consequences that were identified in the risk assessment?

But there is another critical stage, both before and during an emergency, when it's time to look up from your plan and see what is going on in the community around you, and partner with others. (Whether it's the right thing or the wrong thing, we know from the research that most emergency partnerships develop during the response to emergencies rather than before.)

Developing your own plan – that's essential risk management. Forming partnerships during a response – that's essential emergency management.

In Toronto, we started to hear about H1N1 in late April 2009, on a Wednesday. By Thursday, reports really started pouring in about what was happening in Mexico City. That weekend there was a lot of talk among the community health centres in Toronto about what it was going to look like to walk into these organizations on Monday. People started to visualize their responses. By Sunday an online group was established, and dozens of people from across the sector were logging on, asking questions of each other and collaborating on response strategies. It was never in a plan that community health centres would collaborate in this way – the partnerships emerged as the situation unfolded.

Developing your own plan – that's essential risk management. Forming partnerships during a response – that's essential emergency management.

5 Plan for business continuity

Although a lot of the business-continuity literature is written for large organizations, small organizations may face more significant business-continuity threats because of their greater dependence on specific individuals. It is therefore worth thinking through business-continuity strategies for all of the consequences you identify in your planning process.

Take the time to establish: What are the things that we absolutely must keep doing, from a service perspective, or that we must start doing during an emergency? Ask: How manageable is this list of activities during periods of high absenteeism? Lots of organizations say they need to keep doing everything, but must recognize that they're going to be able to serve fewer people. You need to decide how you will triage.

Another important step is figuring out the behind-the-scenes operational activities that must continue or start during an emergency. Payroll, for example, must always continue. If you don't have payroll, you don't have an organization.

Having come up with a manageable list of essential services and behind-the-scenes operations, you can figure out the staff you'll need in place to meet these minimal requirements – a skeleton organizational chart. This allows you to determine whether you can expect to have enough staff with sufficient skills to fill these roles during an emergency, and what training you might need to provide to your core staff.

Once you've outlined these essential emergency tasks and determined who will be playing what roles, you may want to consider sharing this information with your funders. Traditionally, there has been very little dialogue between funders and non-profit organizations regarding suspension of programs, redeploying staff and the need for new programs during an emergency. Funders can be drawn into your stakeholder engagement process as decisions and guesses are made regarding the need for new services and the services and programs that are essential to maintain in an emergency. They may have valuable insights and support to offer.

FIVE GOOD RESOURCES

1. Preparation Guide for an Influenza Pandemic, Association of Ontario Health Centres (2008) (http://www.aohc.org/index.php?ci_id=2768&la_id=1).

2. 'Non-Profit Response to Catastrophic Disasters,' by Naim Kapucu, in *Disaster Prevention and Management: An International Journal*, Vol. 6 (2007).

3. *The Flu Pandemic and You: A Canadian Guide*, by Vincent Lam and Colin Lee (Doubleday Canada, 2006).

4. 'Understanding Voluntary Organizations in Health Emergency Management,' by Susan Phillips and Christopher Stoney, Public Health Agency of Canada, 2006 (http://www.readyforcrisis.ca/resources/pdf/phillips-ep_report-eng.pdf).

5. 'Emergency Health Care Workers' Willingness to Work During Major Emergencies and Disasters,' by Erin Smith, in *Australian Journal of Emergency Management*, Vol. 22 (2), 2007 (http://www.ema.gov.au/www/emaweb/rwpattach.nsf/VAP/(3273BD3F76A7A5DEDAE36942A54D7D90)~vol22no2EmergencyHealthCare.pdf/$file/vol22no2EmergencyHealthCare.pdf).

THOMAS APPLEYARD's *main area of interest is how community-based organizations and networks can serve vulnerable populations during public health emergencies. Clients of his consulting business, Preparedness, include community health and neighbourhood centres, faith-based organizations, emergency shelter and housing programs, HIV/AIDS and other community support organizations, childcare centres, home-care facilities and Aboriginal organizations. Thomas has represented the community health sector on several Ontario Ministry of Health and Long-Term Care and Toronto Public Health emergency planning and advisory committees. Thomas has a Master of Social Work from the University of Toronto, and a Master of Business Administration in Non-Profit Management and Leadership from the Schulich School of Business.*

3

HUMAN RESOURCES

YOU CANNOT manage and you cannot lead from behind closed doors. If you want to have good employee relations, you have to be available, accessible and in touch with issues your employees might be facing.

— David McKechnie

EFFECTIVE HR MANAGEMENT

Lynne Toupin

1 Align skills, knowledge and interests with the jobs that need to be done

2 Pay competitive salaries and benefits

3 Plan for succession

4 Develop and sustain a culture of ongoing learning

5 Integrate your human resources, both paid and unpaid

WORKERS IN THE voluntary sector comprise more than 7 percent of the Canadian labour force; in 2006 this accounted for more employees than in the mining, oil and gas, and construction industries combined. The sector includes not just tens of thousands of volunteers who share their time and talent, but 1.2 million people who work for pay in 69,000 workplaces across the country (this excludes universities and hospitals). This number of paid workers is testimony to the evolution of the voluntary sector from a pure charity model in the early 20th century to the current reality, in which voluntary organizations in Canada provide a vast array of services and programs on behalf of governments as well as concerned groups of individuals.

This sector is characterized by the passion and commitment of its employees, a commitment that is reflected by a much higher degree of job satisfaction when compared to employees in other industries. Here are some ideas for making the most of their enthusiasm and energy.

1 Align skills, knowledge and interests with the jobs that need to be done

Many employees are passionate about the work they do and their organizations' mission. Combining that passion with skills and knowledge is a powerful way to achieve results and drive change. I think of this as the power of alignment: the magic that occurs when a person is in the right job at the right time, making full use of his or her skills, experience and interests, seeing a clear link between his or her own efforts and an organization's overall progress.

By 'skills and experience' I don't just mean what gets described in a resumé. For example, I know of a woman who, arriving from Ghana, worked as an assistant to an executive director for many years. She was diligent in completing all administrative tasks as assigned, but she was also a superb organizer in her community and an astute analyst of public policy – two skills that the organization could have used at various points in time. Unfortunately, she was pigeonholed as an administrator and never given an opportunity to make use of these other skills. Frustrated, she finally left the organization.

2 Pay competitive salaries and benefits

Some may find this controversial: it flies in the face of the traditional charitable model, which decrees that most if not all financial resources should be directed to those the organization is trying to serve.

A study of paid employment in the voluntary sector undertaken by the Canadian Policy Research Networks in 2003, 'Passion and Commitment under Stress,' found that for some categories of jobs, the salary differential between government and non-profit workers was as high as 40 percent. As a result, some voluntary organizations are losing qualified staff to government departments and agencies, which offer better salaries, health and retirement benefits and, in some cases, working conditions.

No one joins the non-profit sector to get rich, but, to quote Judith Maxwell, the former president of the Canadian Policy Research Network, 'workers in this sector are real people with real jobs, real mortgages and real kids who may need support through university.' In other words, employees in this sector should receive fair compensation for their time and talent. They should not be exploited in the dogged pursuit of an organizational mission.

Combining passion with skills and knowledge is a powerful way to achieve results and drive change.

This second idea is indeed a tough one to drive home, especially during an economic downturn or slow recovery. Some may say that employees should simply be happy to have a job – and the unfortunate reality is that some employers in this sector are having to lay off staff at this time. In some workplaces, alternatives to layoffs such as reduced pay and work hours are also being considered. These are tough decisions born of difficult financial circumstances. But at the end of the day, and in a sector dedicated to improving society's collective well-being, it's important that we as employers try to adhere to the principle of paying our employees fair wages and benefits, recognizing the real market value of their jobs, and ensuring that we are not exploiting our workers for the sake of the causes in which we believe.

Most organizations have bright, energetic, capable young people who could assume the mantle of leadership if they were provided with more opportunities for developing their skills and gaining valuable experience.

3 Plan for succession

The problem with succession planning in small organizations lies in the bell curve of age. Many organizations have senior leaders over the age of 55, with few if any employees between 35 and 50 (because most are not big enough to support a layer of middle managers), and then a flock of younger workers under 30.

In these circumstances there is often no heir apparent, but organizations should take a closer look at the under-30 crowd. Most organizations have bright, energetic, capable young people who could assume the mantle of leadership if they were provided with more opportunities for developing their skills and gaining valuable experience. (After all, many of the people now in senior leadership positions started out in their late 20s without much knowledge or experience, either. We tried, we failed, we learned from our mistakes, we got better.)

Another option for succession planning is to broaden the pool of candidates. Instead of considering the talent available within one organization only, why not consider employees from across a cluster of organizations in a given geographic area? This was done some years ago by a group of organizations in San Francisco, many of whom were losing talented employees because the available career ladders were so short. By mapping and considering the skills of all the employees in 50 small organizations as one pool of talent, the organizations were collectively able to support the ongoing development of their staff, keep them in the sector and identify new leaders capable of assuming the senior positions within the cluster as a whole.

4 Develop and sustain a culture of ongoing learning

Some years ago, when I was with the Canadian Co-operative Association, we had an international development program that attracted a number of young employees. We were in the process of hiring for two positions in that department and two interviewees (who had no knowledge of each other) explicitly asked how the CCA would support their ongoing learning and development. Salary was less of an issue than was the opportunity to learn.

Over 60 percent of our workforce already has a college or university degree; most employees aren't keen to go back to school. So what can be done within an organization to support ongoing employee development? I suspect some of you have a range of practices in place to support continued learning. Some of it may be formal (through courses, workshops and conferences) and some may be informal (like mentoring and assignments that stretch employees beyond their comfort zone or beyond their job description).

People who work in the voluntary sector consistently tell us they want to learn with their peers and have opportunities to expand their knowledge of best practices. Every workplace, however small, must reflect on the learning opportunities it can provide its employees.

As a sector, we also need to be better at articulating the knowledge and skills required for particular jobs and providing the tools employees need to better understand the skills and knowledge they have and any gaps they might need to address.

5 Integrate your human resources, both paid and unpaid

This last idea is rapidly gaining prominence in the sector and deserves more time and attention. I'm indebted to Colleen Kelly of Vantage Point for advancing my thoughts on this subject.

Traditionally, as a sector, we have tended to keep HR management for paid employees separate from volunteer management. But the nature and number of volunteers is changing in Canada. When Vantage Point (formerly Volunteer Vancouver) started to see a decline in the number of volunteers, the organization did some investigating and realized there was a cohort of talented people out there who wanted a different kind of volunteering experience. They wanted to contribute their time to an organization, but in ways that made use of their skills, knowledge and expertise. Most did not want to commit for long periods of time and they wanted to be clear about how they were helping to advance the goals of the organization.

Over the years, as the organization identified volunteers with particular skills sets and knowledge, it has strategically made use of their time to help reshape its own internal processes and practices. For instance, volunteers have helped develop a communications strategy, supported the design of a new online system for tracking project activities, and assisted in the transition to a new board governance model. Vantage Point has also promoted this same approach with other organizations in the community. The Canadian Red Cross, a much larger organization, is also a notable example for investing in integrated HR management practices.

Integrating paid and unpaid resources in the workplace takes thoughtful planning and preparation. It can mean ceding some decision-making control to volunteers, adapting work schedules around a volunteer's time, and having more detailed expectations of those volunteers. And, to be clear, there will always be a place for volunteers providing their free time and labour in more traditional ways: serving meals, organizing events, canvassing for funds and so on. But thinking about how talented people, both paid and unpaid, can be effectively deployed in all areas of your organization is well worth the effort.

FIVE GOOD RESOURCES

1. *Good to Great and the Social Sectors: A Monograph to Accompany Good to Great*, by Jim Collins (HarperCollins, 2005).

2. 'A People Lens: How Your Organization Can Adopt a People-First Philosophy,' by Colleen Kelly, Executive Director, Vantage Point (http://www.weinspireandbuildleadership.ca/files/A_People_Lens.pdf).

3. 'Non-profit Jobs Need Better Pay,' by Rick Cohen, in *The Nonprofit Quarterly*, 2009 (http://www.nonprofitquarterly.org/cohenreport/2009/02/26/nonprofit-jobs-need-better-pay).

4. 'The New Volunteer Workforce' by David Eisner, Robert T. Grimm Jr., Shannon Maynard, and Susannah Washburn, *Stanford Social Innovation Review*, Winter 2009 (www.ssireview.org/articles/entry/the_new_volunteer_ workforce/).

5. *The Seven Habits of Highly Effective People: Powerful Lessons in Personal Change*, by Stephen R. Covey (Fireside, 1990).

LYNNE TOUPIN *is an independent consultant working with non-profit organizations to help them achieve clear and measurable results. Previously, she was the executive director of the* HR *Council for the Voluntary and Non-Profit Sector, a national body that works with organizations, educators, labour and government to identify and address issues related to paid employment in the voluntary and non-profit sector. She has led several national non-profit organizations, including the Canadian Co-operative Association and the National Anti-Poverty Organization. Lynne co-chaired the Accord Table for the Voluntary Sector Initiative and served on the MacKay Task Force on the future of the financial services sector in Canada. She has a Masters of Education from l'Université de Montréal and has worked in the field of education in Manitoba as a teacher, school principal, curriculum consultant and special assistant to the Minister of Education.*

IMPROVING EMPLOYMENT RELATIONS

Dave McKechnie

1 X doesn't actually mark anything

2 Walk the floor

3 Constant chatter and reinforcement

4 Meaningful recognition

5 Listen, investigate, respond

A GOOD EMPLOYER and a good manager communicate with employees in a way that is fair and clear. It's hard work that requires flexibility and commitment. There is no checklist to guide you in dealing with every issue – you have to be responsive to individuals and circumstances as problems arise.

However, there are some rules of thumb that can help improve your ability to manage your relationships with employees.

1 X doesn't actually mark anything

There is no map that shows you where the treasure chest of good management is located. In employee relations, 'X' is a moving target and you can only get close to it (you never get there) by constantly focusing on your goals.

One main area where organizations stumble is in establishing proper communications at the beginning of the employment relationship. This is especially true for smaller organizations in which employees are required to wear a variety of different hats: you may have an executive assistant who does HR work, accounting, payroll – any number of responsibilities. It can be difficult to focus on a new employee, but when bringing someone into your organization you must be clear about their duties and the expectations you have. Explain your organization's philosophy and structure, and how you see the new employee fitting in.

However, this isn't just something you do at the outset of the relationship; you must maintain this communication on an ongoing basis. If you're asking an employee to take on a new project, for example, you need to explain the project's objectives and what each person's role will be in achieving them. Lay out the relevant deliverables and the methods you want used to produce those results. (A corollary to this: you must ensure that employees have the resources they need to do their jobs well.)

Another aspect of effective communication: clearly conveying your organization's policies. Few small organizations have written employee handbooks, but they are very valuable. Not everyone needs a legally reviewed 80-page treatise, but every organization will benefit from laying out some basic policies. For example, policies that discuss attendance expectations, vacation rules and procedures for dealing with employee complaints should all be explained at the beginning of the relationship and reinforced throughout the individual's employment.

2 Walk the floor

You cannot manage and you cannot lead from behind closed doors. If you want to have good employee relations, you have to be available, accessible and in touch with issues your employees might be facing.

Sitting behind closed doors creates two fundamental problems. One is that you'll have no knowledge of what's happening outside the walls of your own office. You'll be unaware of any brewing issues and less equipped to respond effectively when you do eventually find out about them. The second problem is that your staff won't trust you, as you will be perceived to be 'out of touch.' In Joshua Ferris's excellent novel, *Then We Came to an End*, an ad agency collapsed, mainly because of rumoured layoffs. All the managers sat behind closed doors and were never accessible to their employees. Even though the company was actually doing fine, the rumours took hold and wound up destroying the organization from within. While this tale is fictional, everyone can think of issues and rumours in the workplace that affect employee morale and productivity.

You must be visible. You have to talk with your employees, know if someone is concerned about vacation time, if there's a harassment issue nobody has brought to your attention, if somebody is unhappy with their work assignment or doesn't know where to go to get help completing their work. You need to be there to keep small issues from developing into destructive forces.

3 Constant chatter and reinforcement

Flowing from this emphasis on visibility is the idea of constant chatter. People who follow sports know that good leaders provide guidance, coaching and encouragement for their players. Throughout every game, there's a coach or lead player who talks to other players, telling them to watch out for a certain player, strategy or positioning. Constant chatter reinforces the players' work, creates energy and momentum, helps troubleshoot and builds team spirit.

You can create this same atmosphere in your organization: engage with your employees regularly, and help them troubleshoot as they go about their work. Formal reviews are crucial, as they allow you to establish expectations, talk about what's working and what isn't, understand what professional development might benefit an employee, and develop plans for how to move forward. Just as essential (or arguably more essential) are informal reviews: it's helpful for an employee to know if she is doing a good job (or not) long before any formal review takes place. An employee shouldn't be surprised at her annual formal review. While the intention may be to motivate the employee to improve following the formal review, the opposite response is more likely.

4 Meaningful recognition

We all want to be recognized when we do a good job, whether we're a CEO or an administrative assistant. Take some time to think about your particular organization, and the occasions that you can use to provide meaningful recognition of the work your staff does.

Pay increases and bonuses don't do what most people think they do. They acknowledge a job well-done, but they are institutional in nature. They tend to come at the same time each year and are a part of an annual administrative cycle. But if, during the course of the year, an employee has done a wonderful job, there's tremendous value in recognizing that accomplishment. It needn't be a showy or monetary gesture – it can be as simple as sending around an email congratulating an employee for a specific hard-fought success.

We all want to know that our hard work means something. When you're talking to employees, when you're thinking about employee relations, remember that everyone on your staff wants to know that they have a stake in your organization's success, that their assignments aren't just busywork but add real value.

5 Listen, investigate, respond

What separates good managers from bad managers in their relationships with employees is how they handle issues when they arise.

Failing to properly respond to issues is a common failing of managers at all levels of seniority. Nobody likes having a difficult conversation with an employee and nobody wants to say, 'You're not doing the job.' But you have to have that conversation, and drawing the process out will only make it worse. It's all too easy to delay, and before you know it you've allowed six months to elapse while an employee continues to perform poorly. As a manager, you are your organization's protector. This means you must put the needs of the organization, and the population you serve, before individual employees. And it's all right to put the organization before the person, as long as you're being fair in the process.

When issues do crop up, respond to them immediately – for the sake of your organization and the well-being of your employees. You cannot let problems fester or else employee morale suffers. Responding immediately is also for the organization's protection. From a legal standpoint, failing to respond to an issue will be held against the organization should a complaint be filed with a tribunal or court.

The first step of an effective response is simple: listen. Engage your employees, find out as much as you can about the problem and get acquainted with the details of what's been going on.

If an employee is struggling, don't resort to saying, 'I really want you to think whether you are a fit here.' You can't assume that the problem is with the employee, that it's her shortcomings that are creating the difficulties. Instead, ask her what she thinks the problem is, and listen to what suggestions she may have for resolving it. Find out what her desired outcome is, and what she hoping you, as her employer, can do to help. Sometimes the changes you make to address a problem really don't suit the circumstances or address the underlying issues.

For issues that involve more than one person in your organization, you must investigate further. Talk to everyone involved in the situation, not just the first person who broaches it with you. Don't promise confidentiality (you can respect confidentiality, but you can't guarantee it); take notes to keep track of what was said by whom; and ask what people are expecting to be done about a situation. And do all this quickly, particularly if you are dealing with a harassment issue: an employer cannot say, 'Listen, I'm busy, but we'll sit down and go over this soon.' You need to react immediately.

Once you've gathered information, discuss the issue with your counsel if there are legal questions involved, or with peers and other managers if you need guidance. There are very few issues that are absolutely unique, and others can often provide advice for handling tricky situations.

After that, you need to respond to the issue – in writing. *Always* in writing as it protects the organization by providing a record of your interaction with the employee(s) in question. This is crucial if there is a chance an employee might be dismissed and litigation might arise. But it's also the fair thing to do and will go a long way in helping the employee to understand what has occurred. Employees should receive written notice when they have done something wrong that needs correction. Include in your written response an explanation of the problem, what you've done to investigate the issue and what measures are to be taken to correct it.

What separates good managers from bad managers in their relationships with employees is how they handle issues when they arise.

The above is by no means an exhaustive guide to improving employee relations – managers must look at their organization's structure and philosophy and tailor their approach accordingly. However, following these suggestions will help you become a better manager and improve your workplace culture before issues come to a head and you pass a point of no return.

FIVE GOOD RESOURCES

1. *Getting to Yes: Negotiating Agreement Without Giving In*, by Roger Fisher (Random House, 1989).
2. *The Office* (DVD; British and U.S. versions). Do the exact opposite of what they do in this show and you'll be a good manager.
3. *Then We Came to an End*, by Joshua Ferris (Penguin, 2008).
4. *Sexual Harassment: A Guide to Conducting Investigations*, by Neena Gupta (Butterworths, 2004).
5. *Best Practices: Employment Policies That Work* by Joan A. Bolland and Ellen E. Mole (Carswell, 1994).

DAVE McKECHNIE *is a partner with McMillan* LLP, *practising in the area of employment, labour relations and business immigration. He regularly advises employers on all aspects of the employment relationship, including employee hiring and termination, human rights and harassment issues, workplace safety, policy development, employment standards, and disability and accommodation issues. Dave has also represented clients in the Ontario Superior Court and Court of Appeal on wrongful dismissal claims, and represents clients in labour arbitrations and at the Ontario Human Rights Tribunal and the Workplace Safety Insurance Appeals Tribunal. He holds a* BA *from Swarthmore College and an* LLB *from the University of Toronto.*

MANAGING UNION RELATIONS

Frances Lankin

1 Know your funding environment, and tell your story

2 A benevolent social mission never (or rarely) compensates for poor human resources or union relations practices

3 When bargaining your contract, choose negotiators carefully

4 Be prepared for external solidarity with your workers, and do not take it personally

5 Adopt a corporate social responsibility model for looking at employee relations

COMMUNITY-BASED AGENCIES GENERALLY need to operate on a shoestring. This often brings them into conflict with unions seeking greater compensation for their members, whose salaries are lower in the non-profit sector than in similar jobs elsewhere. The long-term answer is for both parties to convince funders that core, sustainable funding is required to properly support the agency. In the short term, the interests of community-based agencies are served by having knowledgeable, skilled negotiators on both sides of the table.

Here are five ideas for managing union relations.

1 Know your funding environment, and tell your story

All non-profit organizations are dependent on external funders. Some of these funders are wise, patient and understanding. Others enter into contractual arrangements with an organization to deliver defined services with specific results. These funders may or may not have a mandate to worry about an organization's core capacity, and they may or may not be sympathetic to pleas that a sustainable organization needs a stable, reliable and professional staff complement.

In any relationship, the ability to communicate effectively depends on a common, shared base of information. Employees therefore need to know the funding environment in which they are operating – particularly the leaders of the bargaining unit in your organization. Specifically, employees must see the challenges of managing an organization based on the disparate priorities, timetables and approaches of multiple funders. They also need to understand that the ability to invest in an organization's biggest resource, its staff, can be compromised by these funding arrangements.

Engaging staff in your organization's budget-setting is an essential step toward helping them grasp the larger strategic planning and/or decision-making process. It can also be helpful to involve employees in advocacy efforts with your funders.

Effective communication is not just about conveying your organization's financial circumstance – good employee and union relations require that you invest in relationship building. Depending on the size of the organization and bargaining units, this will mean different things – an employee relations committee, a joint health and safety committee, a well-being committee and perhaps a recognition committee. Relationship building also includes developing an inclusive workplace culture and a shared commitment to the organization's mission.

2 A benevolent social mission never (or rarely) compensates for poor human resources or union relations practices

Most workers in the non-profit sector are proud to be working in an agency that is committed to the public good. However, poor labour relations or a mismanaged payroll will strain the goodwill of even the most angelic employee.

The people who work in the non-profit sector must balance the social purpose of their organization against the bread-and-butter concerns they naturally have for their own well-being. Rarely do people working in non-profits expect that compensation will equal opportunities that may exist in some parts of the private sector, but neither should we expect the individuals who deliver public services to subsidize the cost of delivering those services.

There are other rewards to working in the sector. It is important that these are shared with employees at every level, as they can have a strong impact on morale. Recognition and genuine thanks do not replace adequate compensation, but they are key for building a strong team. Typically, management is very good at recognizing the contribution of volunteers, but recognizing employees is equally important.

It is essential to see your organization from the perspective of your employees, but one caution in this regard: beware of generational differences. Many of us in leadership and management roles were involved in founding organizations and helping them grow; we remember the years when there may have been the strongest emotional connection to our organizational missions. But a young employee, someone with a huge student debt and who didn't share those experiences, might simply resent the poor pay and lousy benefits.

3 When bargaining your contract, choose negotiators carefully

You may be tempted to use community board members when negotiating employee contracts, or, if you are at a large enough organization, you may be inclined to hire an external negotiator. However, negotiators with a strong personal relationship to the parties involved can smooth many inevitable bumps on the road to negotiating a collective agreement.

Collective bargaining is only one aspect of your relationship with unionized employees, a relationship that continues long after contract negotiations have concluded. Ensuring that your negotiator understands this context is extremely important. Be very careful about choosing a negotiator who does not have an ongoing stake in the smooth resolution of employee disputes and the effective implementation of the collective agreement.

It may often seem that the union is bringing in an outsider to conduct negotiations, but chances are that person is a union employee who has some relationship with the local, and may even be back at the table next time. Do not assume that the union's outside negotiator has to be matched by an outsider on management's side.

4 Be prepared for external solidarity with your workers, and do not take it personally

Many trade unionists see the non-profit sector as the next frontier in seeking justice for low-paid, vulnerable workers. Remember that the non-profit sector is performing some functions that were formerly carried out by the public sector. Generally, this has translated into lower pay and benefits for that work, relative to when it was undertaken by the public sector. This makes the non-profit sector a natural target for those who worry about the erosion of decent-paying, middle-class jobs.

Management's job is to overcome an organization's financial vulnerability to provide a public benefit. When you are fulfilling your role as a manager, you don't see yourself as the greedy, top-hatted millionaire from the Monopoly game. It may therefore come as a surprise if you hear yourself characterized as 'management scum' or if you are otherwise impugned during a negotiation process.

The worst thing you can do is take such comments personally.

In so many cases, the reaction of well-meaning management to this kind of positioning has been so bitter that it has made tense negotiations worse, souring relationships with unions and making dispute resolution even more difficult. If you find yourself in this uncomfortable position, bite your tongue: you and the union will have to live with each other after negotiations are over.

5 Adopt a corporate social responsibility model for looking at employee relations

Corporate social responsibility, broadly speaking, describes a corporation's performance in areas such as community philanthropy, environmental stewardship and employee relations. Obviously non-profits do well in the community philanthropy and eco-friendly realms. However, the non-profit sector still has a lot of work to do in developing its most important resource: a more stable, effective and well-paid workforce. Good employee relations and good relations with the unions that often represent workers in the sector is a crucial element of this development.

CSR, it must be remembered, is a business tool: the idea is that doing the right thing can also be a profitable strategy. In the area of employee relations, the research supports this. A federal government study found a direct link between improved labour productivity and good employment practices among private-sector employers.

Non-profit organizations do not have as many resources to invest in the productivity, health and well-being of its employees as do their counterparts in the private sector. The lessons of corporate social responsibility cannot be directly transferred. But CSR remains a sound business practice – one non-profits should follow whenever possible.

FIVE GOOD RESOURCES

1. *Canadian Master Labour Guide*, published annually by CCH.
2. *Canadian Labour Arbitration*, 3rd ed., by Donald J. M. Brown and David M. Beatty (Canada Law Book Company, 2003, with periodic updates available as a service).
3. *Canada Labour Reporter*: newsletter reviewing Canadian wage settlements, cost of living increases, arbitrations and labour board decisions, published monthly by Carswell.
4. *Ontario Labour and Employment Legislation* (Canada Law Book, published annually).
5. Ontario Ministry of Labour (http://www.labour.gov.on.ca/english/) and Ontario Human Rights Commission (http://www.ohrc.on.ca).

FRANCES LANKIN *is co-commissioner of Ontario's Social Assistance Review Committee. A passionate advocate for social justice, she has been a strong voice on community and social issues related to children, youth, disabled, seniors, women and health, and long-term care. For more than a decade, Frances served the constituents in the riding of Beaches–East York as a Member of Provincial Parliament. Elected in 1990, she was appointed Minister of Government Services and Chair of the Management Board of Cabinet. She went on to serve as Minister of Health (1991–93) and Minister of Economic Development and Trade (1993–1995). From 2001 to 2010, Frances served as president and CEO of United Way of Greater Toronto.*

WORKING WITH VOLUNTEERS

Gail Nyberg

1 Communicate clearly, broadly and often

2 Understand and forecast your volunteer needs

3 Have clear and concise position descriptions

4 Train your staff in volunteer management

5 Institute a formal volunteer-recognition process

LIKE MANY OF GANIZATIONS, at the Daily Bread Food Bank we use volunteers for one reason only: because we need to. We couldn't do the work that we do without volunteers. The most important volunteers with any organization are the 'regulars' – not the corporate groups or the school groups or those who come to help with events a few times a year, but the ones who come in routinely and often.

Here are five ideas about working effectively with that core contingent of volunteers.

1 Communicate clearly, broadly and often

To keep morale high, let your regular volunteers know what's happening in your agency and make sure they understand how their efforts are furthering your work. This fosters a sense of engagement and keeps volunteers coming back.

Consider what kinds of mechanisms and tools you have in place to facilitate communication with and among your volunteers. At Daily Bread, we have a volunteer committee in which we discuss programs and projects we're pursuing as an organization, and through which volunteers can offer suggestions and raise any concerns they might have. Whether it's through a newsletter, regular meetings, poster boards or an email list, keep your volunteers updated and make sure they understand their role within the organization.

2 Understand and forecast your volunteer needs

There's nothing worse than having volunteers rattling around with nothing to do, or so much work your volunteer complement can't keep up. It's important to determine what your volunteer needs are, and plan for them accordingly. Recruiting, scheduling, assigning tasks to particular individuals: all this needs to be managed and organized to ensure your organization truly benefits from the volunteers you have available.

As you develop your volunteer program, remember that it needs to serve your organization: your job is to advance your mission, not accommodate every volunteer's every wish. For instance, don't create busywork just to keep eager volunteers occupied. It won't be beneficial to your agency and, more importantly, it won't be beneficial to them.

3 Have clear and concise position descriptions

Potential volunteers must have an accurate sense of what it is they are signing up for – I can't stress enough how important this is.

There's nothing worse than telling a skilled writer that, yes, she can volunteer in the communications department, only to frustrate her on her first day by assigning her filing and administrative tasks. Not because the filing isn't important – that may be exactly what you need – but because the volunteer

Having clear position descriptions will ensure that when people sign up to volunteer, they will be signing up for what it is you actually need.

might resent the mismatch between her expectations and the reality of the situation. Having clear position descriptions will ensure that when people sign up to volunteer, you'll have genuine buy-in: they will be signing up for what it is you actually need. (And don't assume that people with professional skills won't want to do hard labour. I have a former board member who comes in every morning at seven to pick orders – which means putting together skids of food to go to various agencies. He does it because he's retired and he's afraid of getting fat – he says it's cheaper than a gym.)

4 Train your staff in volunteer management

In many cases, the employees responsible for supervising volunteers may need some assistance with that task – they may not otherwise have had managerial experience. This is a great opportunity to provide some professional development for your staff, by offering them management training. It will make your volunteers and your organization as a whole much more effective, and your employees will appreciate the opportunity to develop skills as supervisors.

Informal recognition of your volunteers is essential, but you must also have a formal recognition process.

5 Institute a formal volunteer-recognition process

Informal recognition of your volunteers is essential, but you must also have a formal recognition process. At Daily Bread, staff from every department nominate top volunteers every year; each nominee receives a plaque and a small gift at the AGM. The volunteer of the year receives a larger gift and is recognized in our annual report.

We also have a club for volunteers who log many hours of work. Because many of these volunteers come from low-income households, members of the club receive bags of useful goodies (laundry soap, toothpaste, body wash). In addition, we offer our volunteers free tickets to movies or concerts when there are events with unsold tickets. While individually these are small tokens, together they add up to a system of rewards that acknowledge the invaluable contributions volunteers make.

⟹ FIVE GOOD RESOURCES

1. Volunteer Canada (http://volunteer.ca/topics-and-resources).
2. Service Leader (http://www.serviceleader.org/new/managers/index.php).
3. Professional Administrators of Volunteer Resources (http://www.pavro.on.ca/prof-resources).
4. Energize Inc. (http://www.energizeinc.com).
5. Get Volunteering (http://www.getvolunteering.ca/).

GAIL NYBERG *is the executive director of the Daily Bread Food Bank in the fight against hunger. She is well-versed in poverty issues and was instrumental in pushing the provincial government to support a full poverty-reduction strategy. Prior to joining the Daily Bread Food Bank, Gail served as the first chair of the amalgamated Toronto District School Board, where she led the fight against provincial education funding cutbacks and school closures from 1997 to 2000. During her time at the TDSB, Gail helped create the Toronto Foundation for Student Success, the group responsible for student nutrition in Toronto schools. Gail has also served as program co-coordinator with the Federation of Metro Tenants' Associations, where she advised tenants on their legal rights and advocated for affordable housing.*

MANAGING CONSULTANT RELATIONSHIPS

David Pecaut

1 Understand why you are hiring a consultant

2 Hire someone with the right fit for your organization

3 Determine the deliverables

4 Create a process

5 Get the 'buy-in'

A CONSULTANT SHOULD be someone who helps your organization become more successful. To ensure that you receive the best possible work, you need to understand the parameters of the consultant/client relationship, and provide a structure that avoids common pitfalls and produces concrete results. Here are five ideas to help manage that process.

1 Understand why you are hiring a consultant

There are several possible roles for a consultant. Think clearly about which one you are asking a consultant to undertake, and understand that there may be a different fee in each case.

In one scenario, a consultant acts as an extra set of hands, an additional resource for an organization without requiring it to make a permanent commitment to an additional staff person. To use an analogy from the natural world, this is the consultant as 'ant,' a worker who performs well in the organizational environment.

A consultant may, alternatively, be someone who brings new ideas and social innovation into an organization. This is the consultant as 'honey bee,' helping to disseminate one or many good ideas borrowed from other organizations. A caution: the consultant must understand the environment from which the idea is being borrowed, and the one into which it is being introduced. In this case, the consultant is being hired as an expert whose role can range from facilitating a single workshop to playing a longer-term educational function within your organization.

A third possibility is the consultant who is hired to validate a set of ideas that have already been developed within the organization; what is needed in this scenario is the consultant's endorsement of those ideas in order to sell them higher up in the organization, or to other organizations. This is the consultant as 'butterfly': fluttering around and flattering whoever needs to be impressed. This should be done sparingly and only when the consultant can bring some authentic value to your group. (It is often used as part of a marketing campaign – for instance, to endorse a new set of technical services an organization is offering.)

The last role is the consultant as 'praying mantis.' This arises when an organization needs someone who will bring insight to a difficult problem and will be working in the trenches to help solve the difficulty. This consultant is a generalist, not necessarily someone from a particular discipline but rather a person who brings strong problem-solving methodology and experience.

2 Hire someone with the right fit for your organization

To determine which consultant is the best choice for your particular group and scenario, consider the process you are going to use within your organization to integrate the consultant's work. Are you trying to obtain new insights, or do you need process facilitation? A consultant whose strength is 'content-free' facilitation will drive the process to consensus. Alternatively, if you are really looking for new and innovative ideas, a consensus approach may not be appropriate; you may be looking for a 'content' consultant who is an expert in a particular area.

There must be specific product deliverables, but recognize that the process itself is one of the deliverables.

How do you know when you have found the right consultant? Ask for three references and do a thorough reference check. Specifically, ask for references that are relevant to the kind of job you are asking the consultant to do. In a reference check ask such questions as: How did the consultant help you arrive at a solution for your challenges? How did he deal with people who disagreed with the solution being proposed? How did he deal with you as a client? Is he a content-free facilitator or does he have core expertise in a given field?

Consultants can be measured on three indices:

- ▸ Can they give your organization insight?
- ▸ Do they give your organization impact?
- ▸ Can they build trust within your organization?

If your consultant scores well on each of these, you may have found someone who can align your project's mission with her own passions, become a partner in your project, and connect your organization with others if and when you need her to.

3 Determine the deliverables

Consultants need to have their deliverables articulated clearly. Specify what you are looking for in a way that guides but doesn't hamper them: on the one hand, too many requirements can stifle creativity; on the other, too few requirements may encourage unnecessary digressions.

There must be specific product deliverables, but recognize that the process itself is one of the deliverables. Are you expecting the consultant to sell the final recommendations to staff or to the board of directors as part of the contract? If so, make this explicit. In addition, schedule a check-in early in the process, once the consultant has become familiar with your organization. At that time be flexible in considering alternative approaches to the work or altering its scope if that seems warranted.

In the particularly difficult area of IT consulting, if you don't have someone within your organization who has the expertise to supervise the consultant, consider seeking assistance from someone from a larger organization with whom you have a relationship. Also, make sure the consultant's relationship with IT providers and services is transparent (e.g., that the consultant will not be recommending equipment and/or services for which she receives a commission).

4 Create a process

Your organization's stakeholders and clients both need to be considered in designing the consultation process. You may wish to create a 'phase zero,' where you identify a possible consultant, have an initial meeting to solicit feedback on the process challenges and then revise the process accordingly. This meeting can also give you a preview of how the consultant will work with your group.

Consider different ways to establish process that meets your organization's unique needs. For example, some clients of a community development organization, such as the working poor, may feel intimidated joining a steering group that consists mostly of CEOs of other organizations. A focus-group approach may be more appropriate as a tool for engagement in that case.

As mentioned in the second idea: different processes will require different types of facilitation, and this must be considered in the process of hiring the consultant.

5 Get the 'buy-in'

As you get to the end of the process, check who has been consulted with to arrive at the final recommendations. Identify those who have been missed, and circle back to involve them.

Who will be implementing the decisions? Have they been involved in the consultation process? It is important that everyone who may be affected by the changes your consultant recommends participates in building a common fact base at the outset: that is what consultants rely on when making their recommendations.

At the end of the process, there is always a 'blocker.' Facts may not be enough to sell this person or group on the merits of an idea; ultimately getting their buy-in may involve other, less tangible factors, such as building trust. A good consultant must have the emotional intelligence to be able to realize this and pick an appropriate strategy to get a particular person or group on board: anything from a series of one-on-one meetings to a casual beer!

FIVE GOOD RESOURCES

1. 'Working with consultants,' Imagine Canada (http://library .imaginecanada.ca/resource_guides/human_resources/consultants).

2. 'Techspeak for Nonprofits: How to Communicate Effectively with Technology Professionals – Participant Notes from a Recent Workshop,' Settlement.org (http://atwork.settlement.org/ sys/atwork_whatshappen_detail.asp?anno_id=2006672).

3. How to Choose a Consultant: A Resource for Your Community or Organization, Ministry of Agriculture, Food and Rural Affairs (http://www.omafra.gov.on.ca/english/rural/facts/98-053.htm).

4. 'How to Hire a Social Media Agency or Consultant,' by Jason Falls, Social Media Explorer (http://www.socialmediaexplorer.com/ social-media-marketing/how-to-hire-a-social-media-agency-or-consultant/).

5. 'Tips on Choosing and Working with Consultants,' ACOG (http://www .acog.org/departments/dept_notice.cfm?recno=19&bulletin=1725).

DAVID PECAUT (1955–2009) *was one of Toronto's great city builders and thought leaders. He served as senior partner and managing director in the Boston Consulting Group and co-founded the Canadian practice of* BCG *in Toronto in 1993. He was also the co-founder of Luminato, Toronto Festival of Arts and Creativity, a multidisciplinary arts festival held each June. Beginning in 2002, David was the chair of the Toronto City Summit Alliance, a unique organization that convenes leaders from all sectors of civil society and philosophical perspectives to tackle regional economic, social development and environmental challenges. Under his leadership,* TCSA *championed a series of major region-building initiatives, including the Toronto Region Immigrant Employment Council, the Strong Neighbourhoods Task Force and the Emerging Leaders Network. David went on to spearhead two subsequent major projects: Greening Greater Toronto and DiverseCity: The Greater Toronto Leadership Project. Declared 'the greatest mayor we never had' by the Toronto Star, David succumbed to cancer in 2009 at the age of 54.*

4

RESOURCE DEVELOPMENT

PEOPLE INVEST in passion . . . If you don't believe in what you're doing, you aren't doing your organization any favours, and you won't be able to attract support from funders.

– Paul Born

$ FINANCIAL MANAGEMENT

Lois Fine

1 Your financial statements don't just make a statement; they tell a story

2 The budget doesn't really budge; within its fixed frame, the details paint the picture

3 If you're a charity, make sure you play by your rules

4 Administrative costs are nothing to be ashamed of

5 Smart money cares about a multiple bottom line

AN ORGANIZATION'S FINANCES are like a jigsaw puzzle. There are many components, and they need to work together in just the right way to ensure a balanced whole.

1 Your financial statements don't just make a statement; they tell a story

When asked about their financial statements, most people think first of their budget documents, or income and expense reports. But you can't actually see how much money you have on hand by reading these. You may have surpluses on paper that look huge, but at the same time no money in the bank. Why? One simple answer: the balance sheet. The balance sheet is the hidden gem of any organization. It tells you how you've been doing financially since the day you first opened your doors. It tells you how much money you have readily available, who owes you money, who you owe money to, and how much you have accumulated in reserve. It's an essential part of understanding how your organization is faring. Don't overlook your balance sheet – and make sure you know how to read it properly.

But your full set of financial statements tell a larger story. Simply, they tell you what your organization's priorities are. You can see how much you are spending on program costs, and whether those program costs are for trips to the park with daycare kids or for hygienic supplies for the elderly. The story these statements tell should make sense to you. For example, if your board has decided, after completing a strategic-planning exercise, that you are going to change direction and start investing in suburban youth, you will want to review the next few sets of financial statements and see that, in fact, your spending on the relevant programming has increased. A decrease in that line would be out of step with what your organization is trying to accomplish. Essentially, your financial statements should reflect what you already know you are doing, and they should show changes that correspond to shifts your organization is trying to make.

2 The budget doesn't really budge; within its fixed frame, the details paint the picture

The budget your board members approve before a fiscal year is the budget they should see on every report thereafter – staff can't just go and change a budget the board has approved. And that budget *is* your budget. I can't tell you how many times people have confessed to me that their organizations sometimes use one budget for internal purposes, another when making presentations to a funder, and yet another to a different funder.

Don't do it. First, it's really hard to keep track of what you told whom. Second, your budget is an important tool. It's what you want to come back to every quarter or every year, and use as a way of assessing how well you were able to forecast your needs and make appropriate plans.

Your budget has a large fixed frame – the major elements that don't budge – and then many lines of detail. Those details are what allow you to fine-tune your budget. Remember: your budget is a tool, and it won't serve you well if you can't refine it to meet your needs. I once sat down with a manager to look over the details of her program spending. I found pizza in the travel budget. I asked why, and she said, 'Oh, that was pizza we had for a workshop with teenagers. Our workshop line was full, but we had room in our travel budget, so I charged it to travel.' Well, you can't do that. A slice of pizza is not a subway token, it's pizza – let's be accurate. And since your budget is a tool and you want it to work for you, it's better to show the overspending on workshops and the underspending on travel. When you go through your budgeting process next year, you'll have a clearer understanding of what your real needs are.

3 If you're a charity, make sure you play by your rules

Times are tough for charities right now and they are only getting tougher. Government dollars are harder to get, and governments are turning away from block and grant funding, toward a fee-for-service model. We are being asked to operate more and more like businesses.

Here's the catch: except under the strictest of guidelines, charities cannot run businesses.

The rules for allowable business ventures are laid out by Canada Revenue Agency in great detail. Some basics: if your charity has a business that is run entirely by volunteers, you're in the clear. If your business is conducted as a part of your regular activities (for instance, as part of a training program you run for skills development in youth), you're in the clear. But if, for example, someone approaches your board with some other money-making business opportunity, make sure it will comply with CRA guidelines before considering it. One of a charity's most important assets is its charitable status; never put that at risk, even if a potential business opportunity seems wonderful.

4 Administrative costs are nothing to be ashamed of

We don't walk on water and we don't run on air. Every charity likes to boast about its low administrative costs. Every time I encounter this phenomenon, I wonder why we are trying to outdo each other – not every charity is large enough to benefit from economies of scale. Smaller charities most often have higher administrative costs as a percentage of their total spending, and it isn't due to negligence or improper practices. Canada Revenue Agency allows that charities will incur up to 20 percent administrative costs, yet the norm in the sector seems to be that anything above 10 percent is excessive.

Keep in mind: there are many ways to classify costs, including administrative costs. My favourite example is the lowly paper clip. It's an office expense, right? Therefore it counts as an administrative cost. But think about what that paper clip does. Let's say, for instance, this paper clip collates papers that inform teens about self-esteem issues. This set of papers is handed out in workshops that prepare kids for what to do when they encounter bullying. Maybe even in a workshop facilitated by the suburban youth your organization is trying to help. That paper clip is clearly a program cost. My point: there is more than one way to classify many costs, paper clips included. The next time you hear that an organization spends more than 10 or 15 percent of its budget on its administrative costs, withhold judgment. For all you know, it's calling all its paper clips administrative costs.

5 Smart money cares about a multiple bottom line

You may have heard about the double or triple bottom line. The first bottom line is profit, of course, or in the non-profit sector we would call it the measure of surplus or deficit. A double bottom line measures performance in terms of positive social impact, in addition to the financial assessment. A triple bottom line looks at three measures: financial, social and environmental impacts. And there is now even a quadruple bottom line, with a sustainability measure in the mix, a reflection of an organization's self-sufficiency.

These more nuanced metrics favour the charitable sector, since they value goals we have built into our activities, like improving social outcomes in a community. We can use this to our advantage, by going beyond the traditional grant-based funding models and attracting new kinds of investment. Well-functioning charities have, of necessity, viable, sustainable, people-centred, well-managed business models. And just as businesses historically have, they can rely on this to attract equity and to create opportunities for leveraging assets.

The next time you hear that an organization spends more than 10 or 15 percent of its budget on its administrative costs, withhold judgment. For all you know, it's calling all its paper clips administrative costs.

New money – a younger generation of investors who value social as well as economic impacts, and who are creative in their approach to financing – is thinking in new ways for charities. There are now, for example, patient capital loans – loans with a long principal-payback horizon. There is a growing use of community bonds to finance major capital projects. In England, there have been some fascinating partnerships with government, in cases where organizations provide services that can lower government's own costs. (For instance, investors have recently pooled $8 million to fund three charities that offer mentoring and drug counselling to prison inmates. If there is a 10 percent drop in recidivism rates – which will save the government a great deal in policing, court and prison costs – the investors will see a return of between 7.5 and 13.5 percent.)

Right here in Canada, foundations are beginning to target a certain percentage of their capital base to do mission-related investing. This investing doesn't look for carbon offsets outside of the scope of the foundation – it allows Canadian charities working on sustainable, people- and planet-focused work to be the foundation's local 'carbon offset.'

For example, a charitable foundation may decide that for every dollar it spends on airline travel, it will invest a similar and 'offsetting' amount on local green housing projects or donate those same offsetting dollars to an organization that is committed to doing work on the environment.

FIVE GOOD RESOURCES:

1. 'The Four Horsemen of the Non-Profit Financial Apocalypse,' by Clara Miller, in *The Nonprofit Quarterly*, March 21, 2010 (http://www.nonprofitquarterly.org/index.php?option= com_content&view=article&id=2409:the-four-horsemen- of-the-nonprofit-financial-apocalypse&catid=154).

2. 'Legal Considerations – Registered Charities,' MaRS Discovery District (http://www.marsdd.com/entrepreneurs-toolkit/articles/ Legal-Considerations-Registered-Charities).

3. Drache Aptowitzer LLP: interesting articles, newsletters and tax tips for charities and non-profits in Canada (http://www.drache.ca).

4. 'A New Agenda for Non-Profits,' by Elizabeth Mulholland and Matthew Mendelsohn (http://www.mowatcentre.ca/ opinions.php?opinionID=53).

5. Ontario Nonprofit Network (http://ontariononprofitnetwork.ca).

LOIS FINE, CGA, has over 25 years of financial management experience in the non-profit and charitable sector. She is the director of finance and information technology at YWCA Toronto, overseeing the finances related to the construction of YWCA Elm Centre, an $80-million 300-unit green and affordable housing project for women in downtown Toronto. Lois has consulted widely in the sector, serving agencies, private and public foundations, and government funding bodies. She is the treasurer of the board of the Social Housing Services Corporation Financial Incorporated. An experienced instructor, Lois has taught financial management at the Schulich School of Business, as well as for the Ontario Non-Profit Housing Association, Maytree, the Toronto Hostels Training Centre and the United Way of Greater Toronto.

⊕ TRANSLATING VISION INTO FUNDING

Paul Born

1 Find your passion and
articulate it

2 Get your house
in order

3 Build relationships and then
build the relationship

4 Engage funders in the work
as it unfolds

5 Use your growing credibility and
capacity to build momentum

AT THE CORE of a good organization is a set of ideas and a vision. What is the relationship between the vision you have and the money you'll need? How do you engage funders early in the idea-development cycle of an organization? And how do you build the relationships that will sustain your organization?

1 Find your passion and articulate it

People invest in passion. The correlation between vision, ideas and money starts with passion. If you don't believe in what you're doing, you aren't doing your organization any favours, and you won't be able to attract support from funders.

Before you approach a potential donor, be able to answer three basic questions about your organization:

- ► What are you doing and why is the world a better place because of it?
- ► What do you want to do and how will the world be a better place because of it?
- ► How are you going to involve the donor in your organization?

2 Get your house in order

People do not invest in confusion or incompetence. Build an organization that fills potential donors with confidence. Have a well-developed mission, an identifiable strategic plan, solid financial plans and a process for monitoring your results. Ensure that your organization has the right leaders to implement its strategies. Make sure you have the correct systems in place so that when you receive an investment you can process it professionally. For new and emerging organizations, investing in proper money-management systems (and a bookkeeper) is the single best thing you can do. Finally, understand donors' funding cycles, so you can be in the right place at the right time.

3 Build relationships and then build the relationship

People donate to people they trust. When you are talking to someone who is willing to give or has given to your organization, use the '80–20' rule: spend at least 80 percent of the conversation trying to understand what a funder wants and needs, and never talk more than 20 percent of the time about your organization. Keep detailed notes of these conversations to rely on in future communications.

Build relationships from within your organization. Start by asking your board members about their own relationships with key community members, and use those as a foundation for further engagement.

Large donor gifts require a minimum lead time of several years. A donor's receptiveness to making a large gift will depend on two key considerations: will and ability. Will refers to how much a potential donor knows about your organization and the depth of trust they have in you. Ability refers to the donor's liquidity – how much cash they have available.

A fundraising maxim: do you want a quick 'no' or a slow 'yes'? Be patient and take the time to cultivate relationships.

4 Engage funders in the work as it unfolds

From the outset, frame the opportunity to invest as an invitation to learn. Projects seldom go as planned. Involve your funders as your organization develops and projects progress, so they will be better able to recognize your successes while also understanding the challenges you face. When you hit road bumps in a project, engage with your funders as part of the problem-solving process. Seek their opinions and stoke their interest. If a donor proposes an idea that doesn't entirely dovetail with your plans, don't reject it automatically. Engage the donor in conversation and research potential alternatives.

5 Use your growing credibility and capacity to build momentum

It takes time to build relationships. As you grow, let your donors share in your successes. Involving funders as spokespeople, for instance, will boost your organization and strengthen their sense of connection with you. Create a culture of gratitude within your organization: thank funders, volunteers and staff on a regular basis.

FIVE GOOD RESOURCES

1. *Friendraising: Raising Funds, Finding Friends to Realize Bold Community Visions*, by Paul Born (Tamarack, 2003) (http://.tamarackcommunity.ca/downloads/tools/friendraising.pdf).

2. *Relationship Fundraising: A Donor-Based Approach to the Business of Raising Money*, by Ken Burnett (Jossey-Bass, 2006).

3. *How Today's Rich Give*, by Harvey McKinnon (CD; Jossey-Bass, 2003).

4. *Face to Face: How to Get Bigger Donations from Very Generous People*, by Ken Wyman (http://www.nald.ca/library/research/heritage/compartne/pdfdocs/fac2fac2.pdf).

5. *Fundraising for Social Change*, by Kim Klein (Chardon Press Series, 2001).

PAUL BORN *is the president of Tamarack – An Institute for Community Engagement (http://tamarackcommunity.ca) and has over 20 years of experience in community building, including 12 years as executive director of the Communities Opportunities Development Association (now Lutherwood-CODA), one of Canada's most successful community economic development organizations. Paul has founded and led innovative local and national organizations that have been recognized with national (Imagine) and international (United Nations' top 40) awards in community development, including Vibrant Communities, Opportunities 2000, Foundation for Rural Living and the Canadian Community Economic Development Network.*

APPROACHING GRANTMAKERS SUCCESSFULLY

Robin Cardozo

 1 Show how you can help a grantmaker achieve its objectives

 2 Do your homework

 3 Be aware of the competition for funding

 4 Be open to change

 5 Pay attention to details

THERE'S MORE TO applying for a grant than just filling out a form. It's crucial that you understand a potential funder's expectations and priorities. Are the funder's goals compatible with your organization's mission? Will pursuing a particular funder's money take you away from that mission? It's important to consider the fit between your organization and the funder from the start.

Grantmakers may be corporate, private, public or family foundations, as well as government departments and agencies. Foundations make grants to advance their mission; government departments and agencies make grants to implement public policy. In all cases, grantmakers look to grantees to meet defined objectives. They expect results and hold grantee organizations accountable for achieving them. If an initiative addresses an ongoing need, grantmakers will often want to know how the grantee will be able to continue the program after the grant period has ended.

Grantmakers need grantees. They have objectives they wish to achieve but cannot realize without grantee organizations to carry them out. To a thoughtful grantmaker, a qualified, credible, capable grant applicant is a potential partner in achieving its mission. Approached in this way, the relationship is mutually beneficial.

1 Show how you can help a grantmaker achieve its objectives

Funding bodies do not exist simply to give out money – they depend on applicants to help them realize a specific mission. Do not approach a grantmaker simply as an abstract source of funding. Show how your organization can help the grantmaker achieve its objectives.

Also, be prepared to demonstrate how the initiative will become self-sustaining and remain viable once the grant period is over.

As the application makes its way through the grantmaker's decision-making process, respond promptly to requests for clarification or additional information. This can be a critical time for building and strengthening your relationship. Follow-up questions present a valuable opportunity for you to ask your own questions to strengthen your application and improve its chances of approval.

2 Do your homework

Look at the kinds of initiatives supported by the grantmaker you are approaching. Make sure you know the types of activities it supports, and the size and duration of the grants it issues. There is no point approaching a grantmaker if your initiative does not fit its mandate and scope.

☞ Before approaching any grantmaker, you should have answers to the following questions:
1. What is its mission – what is it trying to achieve?
2. What type of activities does it fund?
3. What size of grants does it make?
4. How long will it fund initiatives?

Avoid approaching a grantmaker 'cold.' If possible, discuss your ideas with the grantmaker before submitting an application. If that is not possible, seek advice from organizations that have received funds from the grantmaker.

3 Be aware of the competition for funding

No grantmaker can fund every good initiative. Ensure that your request is realistic and be prepared to receive less than the full amount.

Consider partnerships and collaborative undertakings to reduce costs and better serve more members of the community. Grantmakers can often point to successful partnerships or collaborations and provide you with an appropriate contact to learn more about their mechanics, successes and pitfalls.

4 Be open to change

While grantmakers do not typically conduct programs themselves, they often have considerable experience in what works and what doesn't in a particular area. When you make an application, be open to the possibility that grantmakers may suggest changes or alternative approaches to your work. They might recommend that you establish a business plan or undertake volunteer development before proceeding with your initiative, for instance. Or they might suggest ways to enhance the initiative's effectiveness, inclusiveness and accessibility. Listen, and consider these suggestions.

Grantmakers do not want a project to fail any more than the non-profit organization does. Be open about changing conditions or shifting needs that become apparent after a grant is under way.

Similarly, as initiatives develop, grantees should provide honest progress reports. Grantmakers do not want a project to fail any more than the non-profit organization does. Be open about changing conditions or shifting needs that become apparent after a grant is under way. It may be that money would be better spent a bit differently, that the project is going to take longer than originally estimated, or that some of the expected results will differ. Most grantmakers are open to reasonable changes, and the terms of a grant can often be renegotiated if alterations are needed to ensure a project's success.

5 Pay attention to details

Success in getting grants depends on more than having good ideas. Your organization must demonstrate its credibility and capacity to carry out the initiative.

Although it may seem obvious, it is essential that you submit a complete and accurate application. If the grantmaker requests a list of your board of directors with addresses and telephone numbers, or an up-to-date budget, or names of references, it most likely will not process an application without this information. Follow the instructions: if the grantmaker asks for a one-page summary of the initiative, do not send a 15-page proposal.

Grantees should also make sure to provide progress and final reports to preserve their reputation within the grantmaking community.

FIVE GOOD RESOURCES

1. Imagine Canada (http://www.imaginecanada.ca/).
2. The Chronicle of Philanthropy (http://www.philanthropy.com).
3. Council on Foundations (http://www.cof.org).
4. The Foundation Center (http://www.foundationcenter.org).
5. Philanthropic Foundations Canada (http://www.pfc.ca).

CEO *of the Ontario Trillium Foundation since 1999,* **ROBIN CARDOZO** *leads one of Canada's largest granting foundations in its mission to make strategic investments that will help build healthy, caring and economically strong communities in Ontario. For 11 years prior to joining the foundation, Robin held progressively senior positions at the United Way of Greater Toronto, culminating in his appointment as vice-president and chief operating officer. An experienced chartered accountant in Canada and Britain, Robin was elected a Fellow of the Institute of Chartered Accountants of Ontario in 2000.*

$ CORPORATE FUNDRAISING

Susan McIsaac

1 Develop a strong, clear value proposition

2 Understand your corporate partners

3 Build support within the company

4 Aim for employee funds

5 Develop meaningful recognition and stewardship

WHILE CANADIAN CORPORATIONS give away a lot of money, securing corporate funding can be a challenge. More than ever, companies are professionalizing their approach to philanthropy and sponsorship, and seeking to align their community investments with their business objectives. At the same time, the number of registered charities in Canada keeps growing, and in addition to traditional charities there are many emerging small agencies that are looking for corporate dollars.

How can you stake your claim and get noticed, not only to secure funding but maintain ongoing support?

1 Develop a strong, clear value proposition

It is critical to illustrate your organization's specific importance and relevance. Ensure that everyone in your organization can articulate the following:

- What you are and what you are not
- What you do
- What your organization hopes to achieve
- Who benefits from what you do and why it is important to the community
- Who would lose if you were not funded

Whether you're presenting an elevator pitch or an in-depth funding proposal, use plain language and offer a powerful explanation of why your organization is uniquely positioned to make an impact on the community you serve.

2 Understand your corporate partners

Know who you are soliciting – both the individual and the corporation. Companies are increasingly looking to be strategic in their community investment. Corporations are leveraging partnerships to fulfill business goals and looking for an alignment of goals with grantees.

☞ **Why companies give:**
- ▶ to be good corporate citizens, because it is the right thing to do
- ▶ to create goodwill and good public relations
- ▶ to respond to marketing interests
- ▶ to create brand value, for the sake of positioning

Find the companies whose interests match what your organization does and find the people who care enough about your mission to invest in it. Tailor your message to your audience and speak to the issues about which they are passionate.

In addition to the larger and more well-known corporate sponsors, don't forget to target small and medium-sized companies in your own community; they are potential supporters as well.

3 Build support within the company

It used to be that corporate executives exchanged 'asks' for their respective causes. While this model of securing support hasn't completely disappeared, the process has been considerably broadened and professionalized. Corporate leadership is still relevant, but there are increasingly more thoughtful approaches to corporate philanthropy.

Corporations are also listening far more to their employees. Companies want opportunities to engage employees and to be responsive to their interests – so make sure those employees are talking about you. Create opportunities within your organization for engaging corporate employees in your cause (for example, special events and targeted volunteer opportunities). Human resources departments play an increasingly important role in creating and permitting opportunities for employee engagement. Cultivate these internal advocates.

4 Aim for employee funds

Employee funds are an important potential revenue source. These funds are pools of undesignated (and unrestricted) monies created through employee donations that are allocated to worthy causes. While these are not officially corporate dollars, they are accessed through the corporate domain. The funds are usually not very large – $5,000 might be typical – but this is a good way to develop a relationship with a corporation. (It is often also possible to leverage matching corporate dollars with employee funds.)

5 Develop meaningful recognition and stewardship

Among the things your corporate partner will be looking for are recognition, engagement opportunities and stewardship. Don't assume you know exactly what a partner is hoping for, though – engage them and ask what they want from the relationship.

Be clear about what you can and cannot do. Do not promise what you cannot deliver (for instance, widespread media coverage). Develop a customized relationship by providing unique and meaningful recognition. Understand if there is an employee component to your partner's recognition and stewardship needs. Consider providing content for company newsletters and opportunities for employee tours and volunteering.

Stewardship can be more complex. Statistical information on financial and service impacts often fails to adequately convey how a grant has affected your organization and the community you serve. Try to communicate how lives have been changed qualitatively as well as quantitatively – try to bring your organization to life. Take funders on tours so they can see the impact of their donations first-hand.

▶ FIVE GOOD RESOURCES

1. Industry Canada's website on corporate social responsibility (http://strategis.ic.gc.ca/epic/internet/incsr-rse.nsf/en/Home).
2. The Canadian Directory to Foundations & Corporations (http://www.imaginecanada.ca/en/node/22) and BIG Online Canada (www.bigdatabase.ca), as guides to potential donors.
3. 'Building Foundation Partnerships: The basics of foundation fundraising and proposal writing,' from Imagine Canada, free with the subscription to the Canadian Directory to Foundations & Corporations. Information is available at: http://www.imaginecanada.ca/directory/resources.
4. 'Guide for Writing a Funding Proposal,' by S. Joseph Levine (http://www.learnerassociates.net/proposal).
5. Doing Business in Toronto (http://www.toronto.ca/business/) and Contact Toronto (http://www.bot.com/AM/Template.cfm?Section=Contact_Toronto).

SUSAN McISAAC *became president and* CEO *of United Way Toronto in 2010. A senior executive with United Way since 1998, she is a key architect of the organization's strategic transformation, from trusted fundraiser to community mobilizer and catalyst for change. Prior to this appointment, Susan was United Way Toronto's chief development officer. Under her leadership, United Way's annual fundraising campaign became a community engagement strategy – an approach that seeks to engage donors and volunteers in community strategies to change social conditions in our city. In the non-profit sector since 1989, Susan previously worked at Ketchum Canada, serving as campaign director for a wide variety of non-profit clients and later as vice-president of educational services.*

$ FUNDRAISING FOR SMALL AND MEDIUM-SIZED ORGANIZATIONS

Ross McGregor

1 Present a clear, concise and compelling case for support

2 Choose the most effective fundraising vehicle(s) for your organization

3 Identify your best prospects

4 Don't be shy about asking for support

5 Build relationships

AS THE NON-PROFIT sector struggles to maintain service levels in the face of diminishing government support, the need for effective private-sector fundraising has never been greater. Here are some tips on important aspects of fundraising and 'friend-raising.'

1 Present a clear, concise and compelling case for support

Potential funders want to know why they should support your organization as opposed to the many other, equally worthy causes seeking their help. These funders are looking for a clear mission statement, a positive image, success stories and endorsements, a sound strategic plan and partnerships with other organizations. They will respond to uniqueness, urgency (but not desperation) and clearly prioritized needs. More than anything, they want to see evidence of the tangible impact of your organization on the community: whom do you serve and precisely how do they benefit from your efforts?

Package this information in a professional and persuasive way. Don't spend money on overproduced, extravagant communications materials that may send a negative signal about your priorities.

2 Choose the most effective fundraising vehicle(s) for your organization

There are advantages and disadvantages associated with every fundraising method. Some strategies may not be appropriate for your particular circumstances. Focus on one or two vehicles that will provide the most attractive return on your precious time, staff and volunteer capacity fundraising budget, and other limited resources.

Personal solicitation: the most effective and efficient fundraising tool with the highest rate of return; relatively inexpensive. Costs $0.10 to $0.20 per dollar raised.

Special events: good for raising profile, cultivating new donors or thanking old ones. However, unless you can attract generous sponsors, events are less effective as fundraising vehicles because they consume tremendous amounts of staff and volunteer time. Costs $0.50 to $1.50 per dollar raised.

Lotteries: prohibitively expensive and risky for small organizations.

Direct mail: reasonably effective depending on your donor base. Get professional assistance and don't expect immediate results. A good return takes several years, especially for new organizations. Costs $0.40 to $1.50 per dollar raised.

Telemarketing: a higher return than direct mail but significant front-end costs; takes several years to develop a constituency.

Online philanthropy: an emerging fundraising vehicle that has been used most effectively by well-established organizations with a compelling case for support, such as disaster relief.

Corporate sponsorship: can be fruitful if you can offer something of commercial value, such as naming rights or other marketing opportunities. Development and servicing of sponsorships can consume considerable staff time, so cultivate relationships strategically.

Public and government scrutiny of fundraising costs is increasing. The Canada Revenue Agency prescribes no higher than $.35 per dollar raised as a reasonable cost for all of your fundraising efforts combined.

3 Identify your best prospects

Target prospects with the highest funding potential for your organization. Start with those who are the most familiar with your work, such as board members, service partners, close friends and current and past supporters. Pursue only those corporations, small businesses, foundations, granting agencies and individuals who have both the financial capacity and the potential motivation to support you. Research the track records and donation history of potential funders; identify their interests and customize your pitch accordingly. Don't be afraid to reach out to specific constituencies that may be especially drawn to your cause (women, ethnocultural communities, etc).

Set specific fundraising objectives for your organization (for instance, that you will approach *x* number of organizations this year and ask for *y* amount of money). Don't be unrealistically ambitious: acquiring significant funders takes time, resources and perseverence.

4 Don't be shy about asking for support

Be professional, specific and persuasive. Clearly explain your case for support. What is your mission and track record? What are your most pressing needs? How much money do you want and how will you spend it? What are the tangible benefits that will result – for your clients, your organization, the community at large and the donors themselves? Customize your appeal to each prospect, taking into account their interests and objectives, as well as your own needs.

An excellent 'asking team' is the executive director or CEO and a senior volunteer or board member from your organization, optimally one who knows the target prospect. Don't hire a fundraising consultant to ask for financial support on your behalf. Fundraising professionals are best used for strategizing, training, mentoring and helping prepare a compelling fundraising package, but your 'asking team' should be comprised of people with first-hand knowledge of your organization.

☞ **The main reasons organizations are not successful at fundraising:**
- ► they don't ask
- ► they don't make fundraising a priority
- ► they hope that their good work will automatically attract financial support
- ► they fear rejection

---

5 Build relationships

Building relationships is the cornerstone of fundraising. Recognize and thank your donors and volunteers – personally and frequently. Continue to provide information to current and potential donors about the fine work you are doing and the critical importance of their support. Share your success stories, and talk about your plans for the future. Seek their advice. Ongoing 'friend-raising' and stewardship pave the way for strong public relations and continuing financial support.

Recruiting board members who are donors themselves or are strong fundraisers is critically important. Small organizations can use smallness to their advantage here: 'If you join our board, you will have a disproportionate impact on our small organization and your efforts will significantly affect our work in the community.' In the same way, involvement in a small organization can also be transformational for key volunteers, inspiring them to become strong, passionate spokespeople for your organization.

FIVE GOOD RESOURCES

1. Charity Village's Quick Guide to Fundraising: an extensive number of articles and online resources on a wide variety of fundraising topics (http://www.charityvillage.com/cv/guides/guide3.asp).

2. *Fundraising for Grassroots Groups: Ideas That Work*, by Ken Wyman (Canadian Government Publishing, 1995). Slightly dated but provides useful, basic information on fundraising for smaller organizations.

3. Imagine Canada's Non-Profit Library (http://library.imaginecanada.ca/).

4. Association of Fundraising Professionals. Membership includes inexpensive luncheons, conferences, networking opportunities, guest speakers, audio conferences and other resources (http://www.afpnet.org/).

5. *Canadian Fundraising and Philanthropy*. A modestly priced twice-monthly newsletter that offers a wide range of useful information for development professionals, including fundraising trends, Third Sector news and practical tips for busy and under-resourced practitioners (http://www.charityinfo.ca).

ROSS McGREGOR *was a founding principal of Ketchum Canada, one of Canada's leading fund-development organizations. During his tenure as president and then chair and CEO, Ketchum helped raise more than $2.4 billion of charitable funding for more than 600 non-profit organizations and public institutions. In 2002, Ross was honoured by his peers with the Lifetime Achievement Award of the Association of Fundraising Professionals in recognition of his leadership in the Canadian non-profit sector over the last two decades. He has served on numerous boards and advisory committees, and in recent years has become involved in several international fundraising initiatives working with Ketchum partners and a variety of national and international organizations.*

DEVELOPING RESOURCES THROUGH PARTNERSHIPS

Helen Walsh

1 Learn to tell your
story well

2 View marketing and fundraising
as indivisible activities

3 Remember that the act of resource
development is really the art of
relationship-building

4 Maximize the usefulness of your
board and minimize the management
time they require

5 Don't forget the
fundraising basics

EVERY ORGANIZATION NEEDS resources in order to stay afloat. How you develop those resources will depend on the nature of your organization. No matter which path you chart, though, you will need partners, funders and external supports to help you meet your goals. For every organization, diversifying its funding base and securing operational support (and not just relying a patchwork of project grants) is the key to stability.

In all your resource-development efforts – whether you are seeking funders, programming partners or other kinds of support – your goal is to create goodwill advocates. These are people who feel they have an emotional stake in helping your organization grow.

One of the organizations I lead, Diaspora Dialogues, is an initiative to help stimulate the voices of culturally diverse and Aboriginal writers in Toronto. When we first started discussing the program and how we might get it off the ground, I didn't yet know exactly what it would be. But I did know the only way we'd make it fly would be to base it on a partnership model: one in which we worked with like-minded people and organizations to leverage available resources and produce a breadth and depth of quality programming quickly, so we'd have a track record that would appeal to the widest range of funders.

So, I met with many people across the arts and community-service sectors for ideas on how we could partner and what, in concrete terms, that meant they could do for us. Could someone co-produce programming? Send information about our programs to their networks? Share insight into who they found to be the most responsive media contacts? Write a letter of support for a grant or review a grant proposal we had drafted? And I always made sure to ask, in turn, what we could do to help these partners in their work.

Even now, years later, I still ask the same questions. Here are five good ideas to help you form strategic partnerships to support your organization.

1 Learn to tell your story well

If you can't communicate your story, you can't enrol others in helping to build your organization. Have a 30-second pitch, a one-page backgrounder and a business plan at the ready to convey your idea to potential supporters.

The people you are pitching to are going to hear in different ways. Some will respond best to long explanations, others to an elevator pitch; some want you to email a backgrounder immediately, and others will consider you seriously only if you have a full business plan in place. Learn, through repeated pitches, which one is the best to trot out in any given situation.

At Diaspora Dialogues, for instance, we have different short pitches depending on whether we are addressing artists, media or community-based organizations. We have short facts and statistics at the ready that we feel communicate the success of our programs, and we always have a personal quote or recent anecdote from a program participant that highlights the real-life impact our programs have – but the language we couch this in depends on our audience. And as I learned from Maytree chair Alan Broadbent, it is also always important to draw the line through to the societal change you're seeking.

Every pitch for support or to raise awareness of your work is a fantastic opportunity to continually craft the telling of your story. Tweaking it can help keep it, and you, sounding fresh – but make sure not to throw out your best words just because you're tired of saying them. You can add new ones to the mix without discarding proven success.

2 View marketing and fundraising as indivisible activities

Everyone who reads anything your organization produces – even internal communications that go to your program participants – is a potential supporter, someone who might offer money, time or in-kind resources. Have your organization's head of fundraising vet all communications and marketing materials to ensure they are tied into resource-development goals.

Fundraising language will always focus on successful outcomes and the societal good or change your organization's programs are helping accomplish. Bringing this structure to every word you write about your organization is time-consuming at first, but a terrific discipline that stays with you.

3 Remember that the act of resource development is really the art of relationship-building

People give to people. Fundraising is all about cultivating your supporters and then tending to the relationship as assiduously as you would your friends, your family or your spouse. Woo organizational partners to extend capacity; ruthlessly evaluate partnerships every year to see which need to be renewed or retired.

Diaspora Dialogues was launched on a partnership model in order to extend our capacity. So we present events in partnership with many festivals in Toronto, as well as theatres, libraries and community centres. We expect our partners to provide free venue space, share marketing support and sometimes share programming costs. We partner with publishers to present their authors (and again to share some costs), as well as with organizations serving writers, artists and different ethnocultural communities. This wide range of organizations benefit from our programming as we benefit from their support.

We have a staff meeting every two weeks at which we review programming and activities, and after every program completion, we evaluate the effectiveness of our partnerships in delivering that program. We also ask

Fundraising is all about cultivating your supporters and then tending to the relationship as assiduously as you would your friends, your family or your spouse.

every participant and partner in every program to fill out an evaluation form every year, and we pick a rotating list to meet with individually for feedback. Between our evaluation and theirs, we decide whether to continue the relationship or not, or whether to institute a probationary period. You don't want to pull out of a relationship too quickly, but at the same time, you don't want to stay in something that is not beneficial.

4 Maximize the usefulness of your board and minimize the management time they require

Your board is there to serve the CEO and the organization, not the other way around. If you are constantly wondering after a board meeting whether it went well, then chances are you feel like you're serving the board rather than offering concrete ways for them to be valuable aids to your organization's work.

If you're running an organization, then you do report to the board. They can hire or fire you. But if the primary relationship is one of reporting, then that can take up far too much management time. Some boards are obviously more activist in inclination; others are more governance-based. Work with your board chair to make clear to everyone what the expectations and obligations are, both for you and for the directors.

Your board is there to serve the CEO and the organization, not the other way around.

When distributing board materials in advance of a meeting, have in mind two clear pieces of advice you want to seek in the meeting. That way, the directors feel they have been of use to you, and you fully leverage the knowledge and/or contacts that are around the table.

Also ascertain whether board members who want to become more engaged are willing to meet individually or in small groups. Find out who is willing to help you fundraise – by writing a letter of introduction, co-signing an appeal, going to a pitch session with you, making calls to their contacts and so on. Once you have determined this, keep a list of who has promised to do what, and follow up. (This is easier if you have a fundraising manager, since her relationship to the board director is less direct than your own, so she can often be more blunt in reminders.)

5 Don't forget the fundraising basics

At Diaspora Dialogues we keep a master grid that lists the grants we apply to every year, grants we plan to apply to for the first time and deadlines for reporting. We also have a cultivation tracking form that lists possible sources of funding that need to be researched – including government, foundation, corporate and individuals – with contact information, notes and next steps for each one. We have a communications grid that outlines what communications each funder or potential new funder will receive from us each calendar year. And we have a stewardship program and tracking form, since it takes less work to get money from a previous funder than it takes to cultivate a new donor.

I've found it important to learn not only what funds are available but what criteria donors consider in their decision making. I try to meet individually with every organization that funds us, both in advance of the application and then after, to understand why we're attractive to them to fund. (I have, alas, found it harder to get those who have turned us down to explain why, except for government grants or public foundations, who will give you details over the phone.)

Finally, every member of your organization should be involved in the fundraising process at some level. Show your staff how their work impacts on, and is impacted by, the organization's ability to raise money and sustain itself.

FIVE GOOD RESOURCES

1. Imagine Canada publishes the *Canadian Directory to Foundations and Corporations* as well as information on foundations and grant-writing (http://www.imaginecanada.ca).

2. Ontario Business Program Guide: Ontario government's free online directory of tax incentives, tax credits and government support programs for business (including non-profits) (http://www.ontario.ca/en/business_program/index.htm).

3. Charity Village offers directories of funding agencies and foundations, plus online tools and resources (http://www.charityvillage.com/cv/ires/fund.asp).

4. *The Philanthropist*: free quarterly review for the non-profit sector (http://www.thephilanthropist.ca/index.php/phil).

5. Philanthropic Foundations Canada: technically a website for grantmakers, but the resources on this website can also help grant seekers better understand the priorities and funding criteria of foundations (http://pfc.ca/en).

HELEN WALSH *has worked for two decades as a writer, editor, publisher and producer in publishing, film, digital media and, more recently, theatre. She is founder and president of Diaspora Dialogues, publisher of* The Literary Review of Canada *(a monthly magazine of book reviews and essays on public affairs and culture) and convener of public discourse events. Helen is a past president and director of the Couchiching Institute on Public Affairs, Canada's oldest public affairs forum, and has sat on the boards of many organizations.*

5

COMMUNICATIONS

BEFORE YOU make a phone call or send an email to a member of the media, ask yourself: Why does my message matter to the public?

If you don't know, it probably isn't news.

– Carol Goar

⊕ BRANDING

Ian Chamandy and Ken Aber

1 Core beliefs, not core values

2 Leaders create leaders

3 Let your leaders lead

4 People don't buy *what* you do, they buy *why* you do it

5 Answer 'Why should I choose you?' in seven words or less

'WHY SHOULD I choose you?'

That's the essential question branding attempts to answer. Unfortunately, it rarely does because it is a highly complex issue that is usually treated superficially. Too many people think a brand is a tagline or logo, when it is actually the psychological and sociological underpinnings of an organization's entire relationship with all of its stakeholders.

Needless to say, there are many factors that go into building a brand that answers that single most important question – why should I choose you? – in a clear, concise and compelling way.

Here are five things you can do to begin to build a powerful brand.

1 Core beliefs, not core values

One traditional way of trying to differentiate your brand is to define your core values. Most organizations invest incredible time, energy and expense in developing a set of core values; typical entries on the list include integrity, responsibility, honesty, accountability – the kinds of moral or character attributes we normally assign to people.

But a few things about this list are a little bizarre. First, all organizations end up with essentially the same set of values, which defeats the purpose of trying to differentiate yourself. Second, many organizations list things such as quality, innovation, customer service – but these are not actually values. Third, the values that truly are values are really just the cost of entry into the human race. Does an organization really need to tell you to be respectful or honest or responsible or trustworthy for you to understand that this is something you should do?

One of our core beliefs (not core values) is that traditional postwar business tools that were invented in business schools and multinational corporations, such as statements of core values, are no longer relevant for contemporary branding purposes. This is true for companies, for foundations and charities, and for NGOs.

You should develop core beliefs, not core values. Beliefs are the basis for how an organization creates itself and does what it does. Defining and publishing its beliefs gives an organization's people tangible guidance as to how they should operate on a day-to-day basis. For instance, we wrote above: 'traditional postwar business tools . . . are no longer relevant for contemporary branding purposes.' This is a core belief that drives us in our work – to always look for new ways of doing things. Core values (and mission and vision, and features and benefits) are vestiges of a less sophisticated era. Your organization can benefit from defining the beliefs that drive your programs and services because doing so will help your people operate in a more focused, consistent way.

2 Leaders create leaders

The primary role of a leader is to create other leaders. Dynamic, confident, effective leaders surround themselves with people who are smarter than they are, then they nurture them and let them take charge in their own areas of expertise. A leader among leaders gets elevated in this process. When you forego an authoritarian, command-and-control approach to managing your organization and instead nurture leaders within it, the results will be phenomenal because you inspire people to make their greatest contribution. And *that* will build your brand, because these leaders are part of your stakeholders' view of your organization. We define branding as 'the relationship between an organization and its stakeholders'; the leadership and culture of the organization is an essential, if indirect, element of the brand. Without the right leadership and culture, you can't have an effective brand.

3 Let your leaders lead

It's not enough to nurture leaders in your organization – you also have to let your leaders lead.

An example: runner Roger Bannister tried unsuccessfully for years to break the four-minute mile. He then tried a new strategy that included two of his teammates: one to lead him at a measured pace for the first half-mile, and the other to do the same for the third quarter-mile. Partway through the first half-mile, Bannister was feeling particularly strong and encouraged his teammate, who was just in front of him, to speed up. His teammate replied, 'Shut up and let me do my job.' This, it proved, was good advice, for it left Bannister with extra energy, making him stronger than ever for the last quarter-mile sprint to the finish and enabling him to be the first person to break the four-minute mile.

Your job is to step away and let your staff do the jobs they've been preparing for. Don't be a micromanager and don't get in their way. But do check with them to support them and hold them accountable.

4. People don't buy *what* you do, they buy *why* you do it

There are two parts to the human brain that are important to branding: the cerebral cortex, which processes rational thoughts, and the limbic system, which deals with feelings and emotions. The problem with trying to sell your product, service or idea rationally on the basis of features and benefits and facts and figures is that the cerebral cortex does not actually drive decision making. It is the limbic system that drives decision-making. So when you're trying to convince people of the merits of your organization, your story has to evoke an emotional response in order to talk to their limbic system.

According to Simon Sinek, a professor at Columbia University and author of *Start With Why*, to generate an emotional response, you have to know *why* you do what you do. Apple makes computers, iPhones, iPads, etc. (the what), that are beautifully designed and easy to use (the how). But what makes Apple really special is that the company knows, and communicates, *why* it does what it does – namely, to change the game in everything it does. What we really buy from Apple is the feeling that we ourselves are game changers simply by using its products. Apple's *why* is its ticket into our emotional brains, the place where we make decisions. So remember, people don't buy what you do, they buy *why* you do it. This is as true for a community organization as it is for a major corporation.

5

Answer 'Why should I choose you?' in seven words or less

'Why should I choose you?' is the single most important, defining question in your branding efforts – whether you're a non-profit foundation, charity, business, political campaign or an individual looking for a job. And you need to be able to answer that question in a clear, concise and compelling way – preferably in seven words or less. This formulation becomes your DNA, the defining statement that runs through all parts of your organization. Whenever you're considering a program, service, initiative or idea, whenever you're conducting internal reviews of your various departments, ask, 'Is this consistent with our DNA?' If it is, that's great. If it isn't, come with an action plan to get that element into alignment with your organizational DNA.

The reason we're using this as the guiding question in defining your brand is that 'Why should I choose you?' offers an easier, more tangible path to clarifying your organizational identity than the more abstract 'Who are you?' But when you arrive at your formulation of why someone should choose you, in seven words or less, you'll find you've also answered who you are. Two seemingly different questions, with the same concise answer.

☞ **Figuring out your organizational DNA will give you five things:**

1. Clarity about who you are and where your organization is going.
2. Confidence to lead boldly and purposefully.
3. Unity in your executive team – because not only will you all be working toward the same goal, you'll be articulating it in the same way.
4. A sense of purpose in your entire community: staff, strategic partners, investors, funders.
5. A competitive advantage. Whether you're hoping to increase the number of people using your programs and services, or the donors who are giving you money, or the politicians offering their support, you will be able to sell your organization far more effectively.

FIVE GOOD RESOURCES

1. *Good To Great: Why Some Companies Make the Leap, and Others Don't*, by Jim Collins (HarperBusiness, 2001).

2. *Creating Passion-Driven Teams: How to Stop Micromanaging and Motivate People to Top Performance*, by Dan Bobinski (Career Press, 2009).

3. *Start With Why: How Great Leaders Inspire Everyone to Take Action*, by Simon Sinek (Portfolio, 2009).

4. *Why Should I Choose You?* by Ken Aber and Ian Chamandy (forthcoming, so keep an eye out for it!).

5. *The Brand You 50: Fifty Ways to Transform Yourself from an 'Employee' into a Brand That Shouts Distinction, Commitment, and Passion!* by Tom Peters (Knopf, 1999).

IAN CHAMANDY *founded Chamandy Computer Services, specializing in the visual communications industries, and subsequently co-founded and spent 15 years running* YOUTV, *a company that developed, sold and managed the 'Speakers' Corner' programming concept. Ian has also designed and executed branding, marketing and communications programs for Procter & Gamble, Bell, Warner Lambert, Labatt, Molson, Loblaws and the Lung Association.*

KEN ABER *has spent his entire career creating innovative strategic partnerships and media programs for blue-chip companies in Canada. As a partner in and president of* HYPN *(now PhD, a division of Omnicom), Ken led marketing and communications programs for Labatt, Cara (Swiss Chalet and Harvey's), American Express and Alberto Culver. He has been a special consultant to Loblaws for seven years and drove the development of its Blue and Joe brands. In addition to building his clients' businesses, Ken has created his own: the Hero Certified Burger chain, which he eventually sold to Lettieri.*

STRATEGIC COMMUNICATIONS

Jennifer Lynn

1 Develop a 'living' communications plan

2 Know your target audience

3 Develop and refine clear and compelling messages

4 Choose tactics to suit your audience

5 Build relationships and strategic alliances

IS YOUR ORGANIZATION top-of-mind with your key stakeholders? A strategic approach to all of your communication activities, both for internal and external audiences, is critical to your organization's success. Consistently keeping your organization visible to all of your stakeholders – including funders, donors and service recipients – is essential.

1 Develop a 'living' communications plan

Your communications plan must align with and encompass your organization's vision, mission, core values, strategic plan and principal activities. Ideally, the plan should be an integrated portfolio of:

- ► public relations (building relationships and generating goodwill)
- ► marketing (building and maintaining markets)
- ► advertising

2 Know your target audience

Once you have a general sense of who your target audience is, learn more about them. For example, what are their demographics (age, residency and so on) and psychographics (attitudes and habits)? The more you know about your target audience's needs, hopes, fears, habits and attitudes, the better prepared and more effective you will be in engaging them in relevant and meaningful communications. Formal and informal surveys, focus groups, comment boxes and website chat rooms are just a few examples of information-gathering methods and sources you can use to learn about your target audience.

☞ **Where do you begin your plan? Ask yourself the 5 W's:**

► **WHO** do we want to communicate with? Who are we trying to reach?

► **WHY** do we want to reach this target audience? Why are we relevant to them?

► **WHAT** is the message we want to communicate?

► **WHERE** do we best reach our target audience?

► **WHEN** is the best time to communicate?

3 Develop and refine clear and compelling messages

Messages should establish or reinforce your brand and the unique character of your organization. The best messages about your brand are always simple, clear and consistent. Core messages should be delivered in several different ways and as frequently as possible. Establish the key words or phrases that best describe your core values and services. An effective mission statement, for example, should be conveyed effectively enough in such a way that all stakeholders can recall it easily.

4 Choose tactics to suit your audience

Develop communications tactics that meet your organization's objectives and are relevant to your target audience. Depending on your objectives, your target audience, your overall strategy and your budget, you may proceed along a number of fronts – media relations, speaking engagements, events and promotions – and utilize a broad range of traditional and online media platforms.

5 Build relationships and strategic alliances

Develop relationships that enhance, extend and take advantage of your internal and external communications capacity – and do so in a number of sectors and disciplines. You may be seeking partners who have complementary client databases or can help you open up new markets. It may be a relationship that offers ways to establish new or non-traditional communications channels to your existing target audience. The key is to establish relationships that enable your organization to achieve more than it could on its own.

FIVE GOOD RESOURCES

1. Canada Newswire: Canada's leading newswire provider, offering bilingual service and expansive networks that reach key traditional and online media and market points locally, nationally and globally (http://www.newswire.ca).

2. The International Association of Business Communicators (IABC): a global network of communicators that promotes professionals in diverse areas of marketing and communications to identify, share and apply the world's most effective communications practices (http://canada.iabc.com/).

3. PR in Canada: daily online source of news, information and commentary for Canada's communications and public relations industry (http://www.princanada.com).

4. *Marketing* magazine: a leading source of news and articles on marketing, advertising, media and PR in Canada (http://www.marketingmag.ca/).

5. Canadian Women in Communications: a national, bilingual organization dedicated to the advancement of women in the communications sector through strategic networking, targeted professional development and high-profile initiatives and partnerships (http://www.cwc-afc.com/).

JENNIFER LYNN *is a communications strategist, diversity specialist, entrepreneur and president of LCI Associates Inc. Prior to establishing LCI, Jennifer was a producer and a broadcast executive with CTV, Canada's largest private television network. She has held faculty positions as Adjunct Professor at Ryerson University and course instructor at Conestoga College. Jennifer is a past chair of the board of the United Way of Greater Toronto, and has served on the boards and standing committees of organizations dedicated to community building, social justice, arts and culture and education. She is a recipient of the Queen's Golden Jubilee Medal, which recognizes 'those persons who have made a significant contribution to Canada, to their community or to their fellow Canadians.'*

⊕ MAXIMIZED MARKETING FOR NON-PROFITS

Donnie Claudino

1 Marketing your organization
is in everyone's job description

2 Stay curious about
your community

3 Discover, continually rediscover
and communicate your value

4 Empower your ambassadors to
reach where/who you can't

5 Reward success and
encourage innovation

MAXIMIZING YOUR ORGANIZATION'S marketing can help reduce the cost of spreading the message about your cause. Harness the hidden power of your community and circles of influence by encouraging and empowering them to share passionately about your organization.

Here are five good ideas to help you maximize your organization's marketing.

1 Marketing your organization is in everyone's job description

At its simplest, marketing is the process of understanding your constituents so that you can create and successfully communicate the value that you offer. Marketing is in everything your organization does: the way the phone is answered, the way your volunteers feel when they are assigned a task, what your donors say about your organization to their friends and colleagues. Marketing is not a machine that is switched on when you need to spread a message – it is in every interaction that happens between your organization and every member of its community, including staff, donors, board members, volunteers and clients. (This *je ne sais quoi* is often what people mean by 'branding.') Marketing has to always be *on*.

The marketing and brand management of your organization might be designated to one person or to a few, but to maximize marketing it must be everyone's responsibility. No one is off the hook, from the president of the board down to the person who answers the phone. Expecting your marketing manager to accomplish all your organization's marketing goals is like the owner of a large car dealership expecting one salesperson to single-handedly interact with all customers.

2 Stay curious about your community

'I've learned that people will forget what you said, people will forget what you did, but people will never forget how you made them feel,' said author Maya Angelou wisely. Stay curious about your community and how they feel about your organization. Commit to providing easy ways for your community to share and communicate with your organization. Offer polls and surveys to gain a greater understanding of the effectiveness of your programs and marketing messages; recruit a volunteer to help you discover and manage other community learning opportunities. Regularly Google your organization, and start conversations with the people who are linking to you and talking about you.

3 Discover, continually rediscover and communicate your value

To maximize your marketing reach and understand your true value to those whose support you are seeking, ask why someone might choose to volunteer for or donate to your organization over another that is also vying for those resources. This can relate to your mission and the services you provide the community, but it can also be a function of much more practical considerations.

If you knew from your volunteers that what they love best about your organization, for instance, is that you offer transportation vouchers and are consistently appreciative of their time, you could communicate that to recruit future volunteers more effectively.

An even greater value to communicate is what you bring to the cause(s) you serve. Where would the world be without your organization? What would be missing? If you had only a brief moment to describe what your organization does, perhaps between subway stops or in an elevator, would you be able to effectively communicate it? Develop and 'mantra-size' an engaging tag line that says what you promise, using as few words as possible. (One leading branding firm based in Toronto coaches its clients to describe themselves in seven words or less.)

4 Empower your ambassadors to reach where/who you can't

This is the golden age of the brand ambassador, where the voice of one speaking to a few is more powerful than a press release sent impersonally to many. Some ambassadors accomplish amazing feats, raising millions of dollars and drawing countless eyes and ears to the causes they champion.

Your organization surely has some superstar supporters who consistently go above and beyond to promote your cause. These ambassadors are the bread and butter for maximizing your organization's marketing. These already-passionate people need only be encouraged to share your messages with their worlds. Arm them with a tool kit of ideas and resources; make it easy for ambassadors to share content from your website and to speak with organizational representatives for guidance.

At the Centre for Social Innovation, an international model for social enterprise based in Toronto, so-called community animators are trained to support the experiences of CSI tenants and guests, infusing the community with resources, activities and energy. Volunteer animators are offered free shared office space, wi-fi, coffee and open access to the diverse and highly regarded CSI community. Create your own community ambassadors by recruiting volunteers to help you *animate* your organization.

5 Reward success and encourage innovation

Someone who really steps up to do something they were not required to do deserves to be celebrated. So do the people who show up every day and keep your organization running smoothly. Reward staff and volunteer excellence by offering tokens of your appreciation: send birthday cards with a gift certificate (donated by a corporate partner); offer extra vacation time; host a happy hour to acknowledge a job well done – and never forget to say thank you.

The non-profit and charitable sector is well-known for its substantial contribution to society, but it is far less known for its creativity, while the corporate sector has laid out many successful models for how to inspire engaged environments that give birth to world-changing innovations.

Push your organization harder to be driven and innovative. Motivate your employees – Intuit's founder, Scott Cook, says, 'People want more than a paycheque. They want to feel as though they are part of something bigger than themselves.' Encourage your staff and volunteers to be creative in their roles. Present the challenges facing the organization to more than just the board – present them to your staff and volunteers. Host organizational brainstorming sessions, and encourage constituents to communicate with your organization through social-media channels.

FIVE GOOD RESOURCES

1. Katya's Non-Profit Marketing Blog (http://www.nonprofitmarketingblog.com).
2. Beth's Blog: How Networked Nonprofits Are Using Social Media to Power Change (http://www.bethkanter.org).
3. *Breakthrough Nonprofit Branding: Seven Principles to Power Extraordinary Results*, by Jocelyne Daw and Carol Cone (John Wiley and Sons, 2010).
4. The Cone Nonprofit Power Brand 100 (http://www.coneinc.com/nonprofitpowerbrand100).
5. Toronto – Cause to Market Meetup (http://www.meetup.com/Toronto-Cause-to-Market-Meetup).

DONNIE CLAUDINO *is the founder of the Toronto Cause to Market Group and the Non-Profit Marketing Group of the American Marketing Association (in Boston). As a board member of the AMA he developed a marketing training series – 'the non-profit marketers' tool box' – to help non-profit managers better understand how and when to utilize marketing tools. He has worked with (and at) organizations in the United States and Canada, including Boston University, Mothers Against Drunk Drivers, Sierra Club, Crohn's and Colitis Foundation, United Planet and TechSoup Canada. He is currently the director of communications and engagement at TechAlliance in London, Ontario. Donnie holds a bachelor's degree in graphic design with a concentration in advertising, and a master's in marketing with a concentration in non-profit management.*

SOCIAL MARKETING

Mark Sarner

1 Break out of the
mission-versus-money trap

2 Know your markets
very, very well

3 Brand your
message

4 Align the media with
the message

5 Invest your money
wisely

SOCIAL MARKETING IS the application of traditional marketing principles to the social sector – using marketing tools and tactics to advance social goals. Social marketing does not require tremendous resources; in fact, the less money you have, the more powerful social marketing can be for your organization.

Why does social marketing matter? Your sustainability as an organization depends on it, because even if you are not marketing, others are.

1 Break out of the mission-versus-money trap

Mission is the reason you exist, but money can become your defining reality. Many organizations find themselves desperate for money and sometimes compromise their mission to receive funds. However, money will follow your mission if your organization has a good social marketing plan.

Your mission must be clear and compelling. It must provide direction to those both inside and outside your organization and explain why you exist. Often mission statements are incomprehensible to those outside the process of creating them. An effective mission statement explains how your organization stands out. What is your unique purpose in the world, and how does that mesh with your goals?

Competition – for funding, for volunteers, for publicity – is rampant. A clear mission can make your organization stand out.

2 Know your markets very, very well

There is a fundamental difference between selling and marketing. To quote marketing professor Philip Kotler: 'The purpose of marketing is to make selling unnecessary.' Organizations can sometimes be transaction-oriented; once they've received a cheque, they view an interaction as complete. In the long term, though, what is important is not any individual cheque, but the cultivation of relationships with funders and donors.

How do you build relationships effectively? Too often, organizations focus on themselves and their missions when communicating with prospective funders. It is more effective to express your organization's ideas in a way that builds a bridge between you and the people you are trying to influence. You need to put yourself in their shoes and figure out what they will respond to. Often, the information we have about funders is superficial. To build relationships we have to create intelligence and insight into who these people are, what they want and what they need.

3 Brand your message

Social marketing attempts to shape perceptions: what people feel, what they believe and how they think are far more persuasive than what people know. To win hearts and minds, a good idea needs a strong brand, and your organization must reflect that branding; there cannot be a disconnect between the two.

Branding is not about advertising and logos – although both are used as elements of branding; it's really about formulating a fundamental idea. Branding builds on a clear vision of what the world can be, incorporating your mission and a distinct interpretation of your issue area. Branding imbues your ideas with purpose, promise and personality – the 'brand bundle.' Those three P's have to be meaningful to your target market.

4 Align the media with the message

Ninety percent of your organization's marketing success comes from the alignment between your ideas and the media that you choose to convey them. The less money you have, the more important the media become. Winning hearts and minds depends not on good works speaking for themselves, but on good works being the assets that are leveraged to get people engaged with your organization.

You should have a systematic approach to communications and make your message as clear and strong (but not flashy) as you can. Follow the backwards planning principle; think about the channels you have and the people you can reach and make sure the media you choose are appropriate. The automatic default used to be a brochure and a poster; then a brochure and a video; then a brochure and a website. It depends on what you are trying to do. Consider the full range of media tools: print, graphic, electronic and personal. Keep it clean, simple and consistent. Focus on content, not on style.

5 Invest your money wisely

The most frequent reasons organizations don't want to do social marketing: lack of time, lack of money and lack of perceived need. But if you are in the social-change field, you are by default a marketer of social ideas. Your real choice is whether you do it by default or by design.

Consider the full range of media tools: print, graphic, electronic and personal. Keep it clean, simple and consistent. Focus on content, not on style.

While organizations often cut back on marketing budgets during tough financial times, research has shown that companies that increase their advertising budgets in a recession benefit in both the short and long term. Your organization's capacity to carry out your vision over the next five years will be determined by how you spend your time and resources now. Making marketing a low priority guarantees low returns.

To get the biggest returns, be strategic. Create core materials that are versatile. Ensure that everyone in the organization is 'on message' and 'on strategy' all the time. Make your environment count; for example, be conscious of the first impression that your premises make. Centralize all marketing and communications to ensure your organization consistently projects one idea in one voice, and that your limited resources are working synergistically and cumulatively.

FIVE GOOD RESOURCES

1. *Marketing Social Change: Changing Behavior to Promote Health, Social Development, and the Environment*, by Alan R. Andreasen (Jossey-Bass, 1995).

2. *Social Marketing: Theoretical and Practical Perspectives*, edited by Marvin E. Goldberg, Martin Fishbein and Susan E. Middlestadt (Psychology Press, 1997).

3. *Social Marketing: Improving the Quality of Life*, by Philip Kotler, Ned Roberto and Nancy Lee (Sage Publications, 2002).

4. *The Art of Cause Marketing: How to Use Advertising to Change Personal Behavior and Public Policy*, by Richard Earle (McGraw-Hill, 2001).

5. *Social Marketing*, edited by Michael Ewing (Routledge, 2002).

MARK SARNER *is president of Manifest Communications Inc., North America's leading social marketing agency, and is one of the foremost authorities on the principles and practice of social marketing. Mark has also been at the forefront of the field of strategic corporate responsibility, and has worked with a wide range of companies – including Bell, Canadian Tire, Coke, Fairmont, Fidelity, Hbc, Kraft, Nike, Sobey's and Sunoco – to develop their philanthropy, social marketing and community-relations programs. He is co-author of* Social Marketing for Business: What to Know, What to Do. *His fund-development clients include Toronto's Mount Sinai Hospital and Providence Centre, London Health Science Centre, Hamilton Health Sciences, Invest in Kids Foundation and the United Jewish Appeal.*

TALKING TO THE MEDIA

Carol Goar

1 Ask yourself why your message matters to the public

2 Don't confuse journalists with publicity agents

3 Do your homework before contacting media

4 Talk about the lives you're changing

5 Remember that reporters ask questions

LET ME START by acknowledging that most communication difficulties between the non-profit sector and the media are on the media side. It frustrates me, as a journalist, that my profession does such a poor job of covering the non-profit sector, which accounts for 8 percent of the nation's economic activity, employs more than 2 million people, provides meaningful work for close to 20 million volunteers, and is larger than many of the industries the media cover exhaustively.

This strikes me not only as bad news judgment, but bad service to our audiences. They want to know what's happening in their communities and how they can make a difference. They deserve to know that some of the most innovative thinking and creative problem-solving in Canadian society is going on in non-profit organizations.

I've fought this battle internally for years. I've tried to lead by example, encouraged reporters to look at the work you're doing, given editors great story ideas and badgered managers about this issue. I regret that I haven't made much headway. If any of you feel as if you're chipping away at a wall of indifference and obduracy, you're probably right. It's not much easier from within.

However, it's also true that I've seen many organizations with great stories to tell make unnecessary mistakes. So I'm going to zero in on five things you can do to increase your odds of getting reporters, editors, broadcasters and producers to pay attention to your organization and your work.

1 Ask yourself why your message matters to the public

Before you make a phone call or send an email to a member of the media, ask yourself: Why does my message matter to the public?

This is the first question an assignment editor is going to ask. If you can't offer a compelling answer, you'll lose this first battle for attention.

Let's say you get past this barrier. An editor might have seen a glimmer of possibility in what you said or might just have a reporter with nothing to do. This editor is going to ask: Why should our audience care about this? If you can't provide a reason, he or she will invent one – one you might not like. It's not that journalists deliberately twist the facts. They have to find a way to make the story interesting. Otherwise it's going to be spiked or buried so far back in the paper or at the end of a broadcast that no one will read or hear it.

Suppose, for example, that you reach or exceed your annual fundraising target. That's a source of great pride to you, your donors and your clients. But it isn't news unless you can demonstrate that you symbolize a new resilience in the non-profit sector or that you've found a formula that allows non-profit organizations to weather hard times.

Or suppose you're providing a valuable service to your clients, as you've done for years. That is certainly creditworthy. But it isn't likely to strike most journalists as newsworthy. If you can't offer a reason you should be singled out from the thousands of other non-profit organizations labouring without recognition, you need to think harder before approaching a media outlet.

As a general rule: anniversaries, changes to your organizational structure and problems with various levels of government don't pass the 'Why should readers care?' test.

> *[Journalists] have to find a way to make the story interesting. Otherwise it's going to be spiked or buried so far back in the paper or at the end of a broadcast that no one will read or hear it.*

2 Don't confuse journalists with publicity agents

If you have a story with a strong public-interest element, by all means offer it to a reporter, columnist, editor or producer. But if your objective is to sell tickets to a gala or lottery, promote your brand, raise your organization's profile or deliver an unfiltered message to the public, that's advertising.

There are cases that straddle the line. A non-profit organization striving to raise enough money to help a family torn apart by a devastating accident, for example, may be newsworthy. But in most instances, if you want publicity, go to a newspaper or broadcast outlet's advertising or promotions department. You'd be surprised how many communications people from the non-profit sector call journalists and deliver what is clearly a pitch for free advertising.

3 Do your homework before contacting media

Get to know who covers your sector. Read the publication or listen to the broadcast you intend to approach. Find out about the organization. Identify anyone who covers non-profit organizations often enough to suggest a pattern – that means more than one or two isolated stories. And figure out how to get in touch with that person. Most media outlets provide email addresses for their staff. If you can't find one, call the organization's newsroom and ask.

If you don't know anyone at the organization and can't see any journalist who shows a consistent interest in your issue or sector, ask around. Other non-profit organizations might offer advice. Your friends might know someone in the media. The parents of your kids' friends might. Use word of mouth as much as you can.

In the event that you have to take the conventional route, look for a phone number or an email listing for the newsroom. Then ask for the assignment editor. Some organizations have an assignment editor, some don't. If the organization you're calling doesn't, explain that you want to speak to someone about a story. What happens next will depend on the organization. You might get a receptionist who takes down the details and passes along the message to an editor. Or you might get a reporter. If that happens, ask if he or she is on deadline before proceeding. If the answer is yes, get a number and arrange to call back at a time when they will be freer from distractions.

Be as brief and succinct as you can. Explain why you believe the story is worth covering. Provide as much lead time as possible. And ensure you provide all the relevant details: time, place, nearest public transit stop and contact number. Ask if the person you're speaking to would like this information in email form.

Though it's certainly easier, you cannot just fling an email message out to the media with 40 or 400 names on the top, hoping someone will pay attention. You have to work harder and be more strategic than that.

4 Talk about the lives you're changing

When telling your story to the media, talk about the difference you're making in people's lives, not about who you are or how your organization functions.

Some of the most interesting and well-read columns I've written are about individuals or groups taking on a challenge that looked impossible and finding an answer, or at least the seeds of an answer; or people combining their talents, resources and commitment to do things governments and the private sector can't or won't do.

A little while ago, for instance, I agreed to meet a woman who told me she had a plan to provide affordable justice to lower- and middle-income Canadians. I thought it unlikely that even the most motivated citizen could crack a problem that had defied

Though it's certainly easier, you cannot just fling an email message out to the media with 40 or 400 names on the top, hoping someone will pay attention.

judges, lawyers, politicians and scholars – but I was curious. Her name was Heidi Mottahedin. She was a mediator who saw clients with serious problems who needed a lawyer but were neither rich enough to hire a lawyer nor destitute enough to qualify for legal aid. Millions of Canadians fall into that category. And it turned out she did have a workable proposal for tackling this situation. She'd already set up and incorporated Lawyers Aid Canada, recruited a top-notch board of directors, and persuaded more than 50 lawyers to offer services to clients of limited means at 40 to 60 percent below market rates. When we met, she didn't want to talk about herself. She wanted people to know there was a place they could go for help.

That's the kind of story that belongs in a newspaper. Readers discovered something they didn't know. The legal community learned about an opportunity for its members to do something about a serious gap in the justice system. And people saw what one individual with vision and determination could accomplish.

5 Remember that reporters ask questions

I offer this as a precaution: remember that reporters ask probing questions, they delve into areas that you might not want to talk about, and they don't follow anybody's script.

Because there has been so little coverage of the non-profit sector and most of the people working in it are motivated by the best instincts, non-profits tend to expect that they will receive kid-glove treatment from the press. Journalists aren't trained to provide that. As the eyes and ears of the public, they ask what people want to know. They raise sensitive issues. They ruffle feathers.

I certainly have. There was, for instance, the time I asked the vice-president of a certain umbrella organization why so many would-be volunteers with valuable skills were being turned away by non-profits they'd faithfully supported for years.

He explained and defended the shift from volunteers to paid staff. I quoted his answers accurately. I didn't push him to say anything he didn't want to say. I tried to be as fair as I could. But I did go to the other sources. I did point out in the article I subsequently wrote that with the largest wave of retirements in Canadian history rapidly approaching, there is going to be a large pool of highly skilled people who mistakenly believe retirement is a time to give back to society.

Some in the non-profit sector were upset and, in some cases, angry. But for months afterward, I kept bumping into people who said, 'That was me you were writing about. I was glad somebody said it publicly.'

I've raised a lot of sensitive issues over the years. I've suggested in several columns that many non-profit organizations have to come to resemble mini-bureaucracies, weighted down by paperwork and constrained by government rules. I've asked the leaders of many organizations whether it was wise to relinquish their flexibility and dilute their message by becoming dependent on government funding. I've watched the charitable sector evolve into the voluntary sector and then the non-profit sector, and expressed misgivings many of you would rather not see in a newspaper.

I understand that this might seem like a betrayal to you. But I wouldn't be doing my job if I ignored concerns I'd raise in any other area of public life. Please understand: I'm not trying to scare anyone off, but there is cultural clash between journalistic ethics and the kind of supportive coverage some might prefer.

☞ . . . And a few media Don'ts:

► Don't use acronyms or jargon when you're speaking to a journalist. I understand that you may need to acquire that language to deal with government officials, but the people I write for don't have a clue what it means.

► Don't contact the media the day of, or the night before, your event. You'll either get the most junior reporter on the staff or no one at all.

► Don't take it personally if a journalist sounds aloof or curt. It's probably because he or she is rushing to meet a deadline, juggling several assignments or wrestling with a difficult story.

FIVE GOOD RESOURCES

1. Pew Research Center's code of journalistic ethics
    (http://www.journalism.org/resources/principles).

2. Non-Profit Resource Management Guide, York University
    (http://www.library.yorku.ca/ccm/BG/guides/nonprofit.htm).

3. Any daily newspaper, community newspaper, ethnic newspaper,
    local television or radio station. Try to identify who, if anyone,
    shows a consistent interest in social justice, the environment,
    culture or amateur sport.

4. A couple of examples of effective storytelling in the *Toronto Star*
    by Carol Goar:

    ▶ 'One Woman's Crusade for Affordable Justice' (http://www.thestar
    .com/article/758007--one-woman-s-crusade-for-affordable-justice)

    ▶ 'Sharing a Passion to Make a Difference' (http://www.thestar.com/
    opinion/article/750967--sharing-a-passion-to-make-a-difference)

5. Pitching Your Story to the Media, a workshop with Jennifer
    Lewington and Julia Howell that explored distilling complex
    stories into effective news items (http://maytree.com/training/
    annual-conference/2009-conference/resources#workshops).

CAROL GOAR *has been a journalist for 35 years. She began her career as an
economics reporter at the* Ottawa Citizen, *then moved to Parliament Hill as
a reporter for the Canadian Press, the* Toronto Star, *and Maclean's magazine. The* Star *invited her back to be its national affairs columnist and she has
stayed at the newspaper ever since. After ten years Carol moved to Washington
to become United States bureau chief, and she finally returned to Toronto as
editorial page editor. Carol has now returned to her first love: writing. She tries
to bring attention to neglected issues and highlight the efforts of those striving
to make a difference. Carol is also a trustee of the Atkinson Foundation.*

 # WEB 2.0

Jason Mogus

1 Stories matter

2 Give to get

3 Let go of control

4 Try new things, take some risks, and focus on your core offerings

5 Integrate network thinking into your internal processes

IT'S TIME TO change how you view the internet. The web is more than an online brochure; it represents your entire organization to the world. Increasingly, it's the primary channel where your audiences and stakeholders are hearing about you, getting information and getting things done.

Your online presence is not happening only on your website: digital is everywhere your brand or your issues play out in your constituents' lives – through social media, on other websites where they spend time, in the blogosphere and on traditional media sites, on mobile phones and more. Smart organizations manage across many different channels, and view the web as a network, not a node.

Web 1.0, the first phase of the internet's development, was about publishing. This meant getting information out to more and more people and improving access to knowledge. Web 2.0, however, is a conversation; it focuses on networks, interactions and relationships. Web 2.0 has introduced exciting changes and questions into online communications; you now have many more tools at your disposal for discovering and engaging with your audiences. How can you involve others in meaningful ways in your work and break down traditional barriers? How can the web help you listen and learn? And how can you work within an ecosystem of other organizations to achieve success that serves the whole? Some people are still trying to manipulate Web 2.0 as they did Web 1.0, by using it to push out more information and reach more people. Ultimately this will fail, because a conversation has to be multidirectional.

Every organization I've worked with has wanted to achieve more or less the same things:

- reach more people
- engage the public in new ways
- raise more funds
- collaborate and share knowledge with peers more effectively
- understand the changing world around them better
- receive feedback on how they are doing
- have an impact on their mission.

What I've found is that web tools can help organizations and the people inside and outside them become more connected, collaborative, innovative and effective. The web is a major force driving bigger cultural changes. And since the web is a network, organizations that think and move like a network are seeing the most success – online and in the real world.

☛ **Quick overview of Web 2.0 tools**
- Blogs: expressing and engaging. Blogs unlock the door to an insider's view of our organizations, their successes and failures. Most blogs also give the reader an opportunity to respond.
- Rich media: compelling storytelling. This is about using podcasts and video to tell stories and put out your message.
- Social networking (Facebook, Twitter, LinkedIn, etc.): building relationships and making connections.
- Social bookmarks and wikis: knowledge sharing and collaborating.
- Online communities: tying it all together.

These tools can help you. But for them to be successful you need to change the *culture* of your organization, and the way you think. You need to shift to 'web thinking,' which values:

- Collaboration: inside organizations, among organizations and across sectors. This isn't always easy, but it can produce fantastic results.
- Transparency: being authentic and accessible. You do not always have to present a polished, finished product to the outside world. Being upfront about difficulties and weakness makes you more vulnerable, but it also makes you more real.

- Participation: meaningfully engaging people, especially new people, in your work.
- Listening: being open, soliciting feedback and being ready to hear what comes back. There's no point in engaging people if you make decisions independently of their responses.

If you don't employ this approach, you may have all the technology in the world and achieve little success. I have found that what works on the web is what works in living systems. The behaviours, techniques and mindset behind the web are the same as those behind successful social change.

Here are five good ideas for incorporating Web 2.0 tools into your organization.

1 Stories matter

Speak passionately about the things that matter to you and give voice to those you serve. Tell your stories better, and if you can't, due to a lack of capacity or funding, partner with people who can.

With the blossoming of new digital channels over the past few years, one thing remains true across all of them: content is still king. Audiences expect a different kind of storytelling these days, and if you don't compel them, quickly, about the big ideas behind your service, cause or campaign, you miss your opportunity to connect.

An integrated content strategy, grown from your deepest areas of expertise, tied to your positioning and strategic goals, and rolled out differently across different platforms, will ensure that your mediums support – rather than compete with – each other. The good news? If you settle on a few key messages relevant to your audiences and repeat them in creative ways in multiple media, you will break through.

Storytelling can be taught if it's made a priority for staff. And doing it in the digital age is much less expensive than when you had to rely on traditional media. Some tips:

- Balance your data with stories. Research has shown that people are more affected by stories than data.
- Get creative! Podcasts, videos and flash movies are all likely to grab the attention of your audience.
- Tell stories about solutions and outcomes, not issues or your campaigns.

2 Give to get

If your organization is serious about Web 2.0, it has to be committed to the process and prepared to make the investment, in both time and resources. A half-hearted attempt is bound to fail. This means an initial investment in setting up the tools you need, and then ongoing attention to ensure you keep your participation vibrant and engaged. It isn't enough to just set up a blog or Facebook page – you need to interact with the people who visit it, and actively reach out to people whose interests overlap with yours.

To have a high-performing digital program, first make sure there is a coherent and clear connection between your digital strategies and tactics and your core organizational goals, messages, campaigns and priorities. Ensure that business goals from not only marketing but all key departments are driving changes to digital, and sharing in the investment. And, importantly, track performance with clear, non-technical metrics that make sense to those in other departments, so ideally they can co-own them. Digital supports everyone, so everyone needs to pay attention to how it is helping them succeed.

Make sure there is a coherent and clear connection between your digital strategies and tactics and your core organizational goals, messages, campaigns and priorities.

Here are some questions to ask yourself as you revisit your online strategy:

- ► Why are you online/in social media/using email? How does this support the core mission and goals of your organization?
- ► How closely do your current channels reflect the most exciting and successful areas of your business? Are resources overinvested in legacy programs at the expense of emerging ones?

- ▶ What key performance indicators for digital are you tracking? Are they communicated to senior leaders across departments to create excitement and co-ownership of outcomes?

3 Let go of control

Putting information into the public domain and inviting comment is a risk – one you must be prepared to make. While it is natural to want to mitigate the risks of exposure, there will undoubtedly be a shift in power and control from your organization toward its audience and clients.

Collaborate, don't dominate the agenda. Ask for help. Trust that your audience has something useful to offer. You'll be amazed at the results.

4 Try new things, take some risks and focus on your core offerings

Be flexible in your approach and don't be afraid of failing: you will learn from your failures and move forward. Likewise, don't expect perfection from others, especially on the first attempt.

Find a way to integrate new energy from different movements and sectors. Young people may have more ideas and enthusiasm for new technologies; likewise, the corporate sector may be more advanced. Invite people from these demographics on board and get some feedback and fresh opinions about your online ventures. Seek out audiences who don't agree with you or don't 'get' you. Their feedback will yield important information on how you can make your programs more relevant to their worlds.

Capital follows ideas, success and results.

Take it one step at a time and seek excellence in everything you do. Don't profile every program you've ever offered. Instead, promote what is working well and has the most vitality and momentum.

Bear in mind that the default state of most online communities – or any online innovation project – is often failure. So ensure that you are asking for help from others, engaging advisors and stakeholders, and getting as much feedback as possible. Don't be afraid of negative feedback, as this is likely to help you more than positive feedback. Trust that new sources of funding and support will emerge. Capital follows ideas, success and results.

5 Integrate network thinking into your internal processes

Digital strategies aren't just for communication with external stakeholders; technology can facilitate collaboration, productivity and knowledge sharing within your organization as well. Tools like wikis, data collection, management software, dashboards, social bookmarking and crowdsourcing can streamline co-operative efforts, document institutional memory and rally your team members around shared goals and interests – and do so both within and across departments.

Forward-looking organizations are bringing these tools to bear on a plethora of management challenges. A well-developed dashboard, for instance, can be used to visualize key metrics in ways we might previously have seen only in splashy annual reports; and wikis are housing information that used to be lost whenever staff turned over. While it's critical to integrate digital media into your external communications, it's equally fundamental to provide your staff with digital tools that help them do their work better, whether it's program delivery, campaigns, fundraising or even traditional communications work like media outreach and advertising.

FIVE GOOD RESOURCES

1. Text-based definition of Web 2.0: Wikipedia has the classic definition (http://en.wikipedia.org/wiki/Web_2.0), but this one, while a bit more technical, is rich with meaning: http://edgeperspectives.typepad.com/edge_perspectives/2005/09/what_is_web_20.html.

2. Video definition: the most well-known overview of Web 2.0 is an easy-to-watch four-minute video, 'The Machine Is Us/ing Us': http://www.youtube.com/watch?v=6gmP4nkoEOE.

3. *Getting to Maybe: How the World Is Changed*, by Frances Westley, Brenda Zimmerman and Michael Quinn Patton (Vintage, 2007).

4. *Leadership and the New Science: Learning About Organizations from an Orderly Universe*, by Margaret Wheatley (Berrett-Koehler, 1992).

5. Conference: Web of Change at Hollyhock (http://webofchange.com).

JASON MOGUS *is the* CEO *and principal strategist at Communicopia, a Webby Award–winning digital consultancy that helps social-mission organizations adapt to a networked world by creating high-performance digital campaigns, sites and teams. Jason has led digital transformation projects for the TckTckTck global climate-change campaign, The Elders, Natural Resources Defense Council, Make Poverty History, the United Nations Foundation and the City of Vancouver. He is also the founder of the Web of Change, a community of senior leaders working at the convergence of technology, organizing and social change. Jason was a founding partner and board member with B.C. Social Venture Partners, a founding board member of Canadian Business for Social Responsibility, and is a long-time member of the Social Venture Network in the U.S.*

⊕ BUILDING CONVERSATIONS ON THE WEB

Marco Campana and Christopher Wulff

1 Online conversations are still conversations

2 Integrate your online and offline work

3 Don't let the technology become the conversation

4 Your conversations will evolve; be prepared to evolve with them

5 Don't just innovate – participate

THE HYPE: online communications change every paradigm, and people who don't get it will be left behind.

The reality: we're social animals and we've been communicating as long as we've been around. We knew how to talk to each other before the internet.

The key: You already know how to do this. Don't go online and forget everything you already know.

The web has the potential to return us to the best of community development, public education and local organizing traditions. It is by nature non-hierarchical, democratic and decentralized, with information and opinion flowing easily between whoever chooses to participate.

The following five good ideas are principles we think are important for conversations and service delivery online. Start by recognizing the skills and knowledge you already hold, translate them into this new context, and explore how the principles of community and group development provide a road map to building conversations on the web.

1 Online conversations are still conversations

You're already having conversations, engaging community, providing service. You already know about community development and engagement.

Conversations online are no different from conversations offline. When you hear about an online discussion forum, think of a drop-in centre or workshop, a place where people come for help and social connection with whoever else is in the room. When you hear about instant messaging and email, think about a one-on-one counselling session. When you hear about eLearning, go back to your workshops and training. Some conversations happen one-on-one; some happen in small groups led by you as moderator or facilitator; and some are community conversations, unmoderated, with you as another community member.

Online conversations are participative approaches to service delivery. You have to be prepared to contribute, share power, be accountable and be present and available.

More and more, your clients will expect this of you, both online and offline.

2 Integrate your online and offline work

The number one recipe for disaster in any attempt at online engagement is to not take it seriously. It takes resources, it takes time and it takes thoughtful planning. Just as with any other conversation or engagement process, you need to determine who you are trying to talk to (or with) and what you want to talk about, and then you need to seed the conversation and nurture it to encourage participation.

Technology and e-service delivery are useful to complement relationships that are already in progress. Think of it as hybrid service delivery: if you have a partner, service provider, client or colleague you often meet with in person, maybe there's a way to save travel time and expedite planning by interacting online part of the time. This can be by email (which we often don't think of as an online service), via a social network, or on Twitter or Skype. What matters isn't how cool or new the technology is, but that it works for you and your partners.

This doesn't mean you decrease

Just as with any other conversation, you need to determine who you are trying to talk to (or with) and what you want to talk about, and then you need to seed the conversation and nurture it to encourage participation.

human interactions either. Far from it. You're offering service choice for your clients, in a way you may not have previously been able to.

If you start a discussion forum, tell people about it! Highlight it on the front page of your website, saying, 'Come ask us questions.' But be prepared to actively participate. Because the moment someone asks a question and you don't respond for four days, you've lost that connection. Don't create online outposts and then let them turn to tumbleweeds. You wouldn't ignore the phone or clients who walk in the front door. Don't make that mistake online.

The best way to get your organization thinking seriously about integrating effective online communication is to embed it into every part of what you're doing, and into your organization's day-to-day work. Staff are already using technology in their service work – they just may not yet define it as community building, or client service work.

Some important questions to ask yourself: How can we complement existing service delivery and offer clients another way to get help? Can online, interactive access to – and connection with – counsellors, information, mentors and advisors, peers and other learning resources be part of a service solution?

Set some important principles, such as:

- no loss of human-service interaction with clients
- minimal increase in workload for staff; instead, a change in how you work with some of your clients
- online work must complement existing services
- online work must contribute to meeting client service targets
- online service is not for all clients
- privacy and confidentiality are essential
- maintaining a high level of client-centric service focus is essential

3 Don't let the technology become the conversation

Don't just run out and play with the latest technological innovation. There are plenty of non-profit and charity technology experts who will do that for you. Let them be the early adopters. learn from them, then decide if it makes sense for you to invest time and resources in a particular tool. But never forget your immediate questions: Are your clients using this technology? If they're not, why would you? That would be like opening an office in a place where none of your clients live.

It's hard to isolate technology from the conversations you have via that technology. Often people talk about the tools themselves rather than about how those tools can change lives, change service delivery. Don't let the technology become the conversation with your community.

Don't say: 'Like us on Facebook!' Say: 'This is what we can do for you. We can do some of that on Facebook now too!'

If you decide to use a wiki for collaborative work, don't call it a wiki. If you do, you just made it about the technology. People will wonder what a wiki is, not how they can use it to collaborate. They don't have to know what it is, it just has to work for them. Most people are not interested in what the technology is, they just want to know how they can use it. For most of us, technology is just a means to an end.

Are your clients using this technology? If they're not, why would you? That would be like opening an office in a place where none of your clients live.

4 Your conversations will evolve; be prepared to evolve with them

The original reasons you started or participated in an online conversation may evolve over time. Others may take control as you shift from owner to participant at times, discussions may move in and out of your online space and across/between other sites, your role may change from information hub or sector expert to facilitator or collaborator. For some people in some organizations this means ceding some control. That's not always easy. But it is community building.

Enthusiasts can dominate online conversations. It happens whenever you run a group offline, doesn't it? Be prepared for this. You're managing group dynamics. It's the same thing online. Try to harness that enthusiasm.

Online conversations tend to follow the 90-9-1 rule: 90 percent of people are lurkers, 9 percent are commenting, and 1 percent are your most frequent contributors. It's web theatre, because 90 percent of your audience may not be actively participating, but they are watching. You are talking to them, indirectly, by engaging in conversations with frequent contributors. They are paying attention to these interactions. When you respond to people online, you're also responding to the same quiet people who never raise their hands.

5 Don't just innovate – participate

What would you do when starting a new program in your agency? Some sort of a needs assessment, right? You'd find out as much about your clients and community as you could. It's no different online.

If your clients congregate at temple, a cultural centre, the library, you meet them there. Do the same thing online. Speak to people where and how and when they want to be spoken with. Don't create 'yet another website' or 'another place to go' if one isn't necessary.

You will always have an online home – your website, blog, etc. And, yes, you want people to come there. But what matters more is that you create or become part of a space that your clients consider a trusted network, and that you show them you can also meet them in their spaces. This might involve commenting on other websites, or joining message boards you are not administering.

In the end, it's not about the technology, and it's not about the person who is controlling the technology. It's all about you – your presence, your identity, your ideas and your network.

FIVE GOOD RESOURCES

1. *Design for Community*, by Derek M. Powazek (Waite Group, 2001).
2. *Mobilizing Generation 2.0: A Practical Guide to Using Web 2.0 Technologies to Recruit, Organize and Engage Youth*, by Ben Rigby (Jossey-Bass, 2008).
3. TechSoup Canada (http://www.techsoupcanada.ca).
4. My Charity Connects (http://mycharityconnects.org).
5. Fresh Networks, Community Management posts (http://www.freshnetworks.com/blog/category/topics/onlinecommunities/).

MARCO CAMPANA's *work has spanned several non-profit sectors, including newcomer settlement, employment, information and referral, and community-based internet projects. Before joining Maytree as a communications strategist, where he helps staff harness the potential of the web and social media, Marco worked as a website content coordinator and, more recently, provided social media training and support for the settlement sector in Ontario.*

CHRISTOPHER WULFF *has spent the last ten years working with non-profits across Ontario on integrating technology into their services, operations and communications. Whether his role is graphic designer, project planner or web developer, his goals are always to find the most effective and appropriate solution to any problem. He currently does this work through Patience and Fortitude, a small consulting and development firm he founded, while also pursuing his Master's of Divinity from the University of Toronto.*

SUCCESSFUL NETWORKING

Lisa Mattam

1 Know your brand

2 Build your message

3 Develop a map

4 Be consistent

5 Embrace the unexpected

NETWORKING IS MUCH more than 'working a room.' It is a state of mind, an attitude you layer onto the jobs you do every day. Networking should be present in everything you do.

1 Know your brand

In my previous life, I was a pharmaceutical marketer. We learned quickly as brand managers that people choose products and services based on the attributes they associate with a brand. As a marketer you spend a lot of time grasping the nuances of this dynamic: figuring out what your brand's essence is, what people can become attached to, what they can believe in, why they choose you.

It's easy to see this if you think about your own life, and the everyday choices you make. When you choose a dry cleaner or a hair stylist or a financial adviser, you choose them because of some characteristic you believe they exemplify – that they are more convenient or consistent or astute than the other candidates you were considering. As a networker, you can define what that one thing is for you, that distinctive quality that you exemplify. You need to define that attribute, and you need a way of capturing that, distilling it so you can convey it in 30 seconds and begin to market your brand.

2 Build your message

Networking isn't just about sharing your brand; it relies on having a specific message to convey. You need to be guided by an intention – there must be something you're hoping to accomplish with each interaction, and you need to communicate that intention effectively to increase the chances that people will respond to you.

Networking can have several different purposes. One is what author Tim Cork calls 'net-giving' – offering something that might help someone out in the course of networking. A second is the inverse – asking for assistance from someone you already know and with whom you're already comfortable. But the third is the one that most often comes to mind when we think about networking: the 'I want to keep you within my network' kind of interaction. What does that really mean? A more concrete message can be something as simple as 'It was really great meeting you today. I'd love to get together for a coffee, maybe once every six months, and exchange ideas about some of the programs we're each running and how we might be able to help each other in our work.' Suddenly there's some intent, there's a course of action to pursue.

3 Develop a map

People increasingly rely on social media tools like Facebook or LinkedIn to keep track of their colleagues and professional acquaintances, but these don't give you a robust sense of your network. What I suggest you do is map out your network, in order to really understand it. Take a blank sheet of paper, put your name in the middle, and create branches extending from it. You can put anybody you want on those branches: colleagues, family members, your dentist – anyone with whom you have a genuine connection. That's the key: the people you include must be ones you could talk to about your career, your organization, your extra-curricular activities. And then look at those individuals, and start making branches out of them, filling in more details. This is your network map.

The first contrast you'll see between your network as captured on your map and the way you're used to seeing it on social media platforms like Facebook is its size. In your network map, if someone isn't able to support you in your professional activities, they can't make the list. You're cutting out all the incidental five-minute conversations that lead to LinkedIn connections but then never progress, and adding all the people who can be helpful but might not be using these social media platforms. (LinkedIn is a fabulous tool but the point is not to use LinkedIn as a crutch.)

The second element you'll glean from your map is a sense of how interconnected your network is. Once you have the names down, draw lines to show relationships between people who know each other. What you might find is that your network is so interconnected that everybody knows each other. This is a natural but limiting element of networks: it isn't that the people you know (and the people they know) aren't valuable, but if your network is very interconnected, you're constantly getting access to the same pool of people rather than expanding into new areas.

The third element of your network map is diversity. Are most of your contacts are from the same industry, school, institution or area of specialization? A robust network needs to include people from a variety of sectors.

4 Be consistent

Consistency is important with networking. People want to be able to rely on you; they want to know that no matter how many times they call, they will always get a response, that when you say you'll follow up on a matter you will. That's what makes people want to keep you in their network: a tangible connection they can depend on.

We already know that 70 percent of new businesses and 60 percent of new jobs are generated through some sort of networking. What is mentioned less often is that most of those things don't come from your immediate network. They come from different layers of your network map. That's why the network map is important. It might not be the person you immediately know who helps you out, but someone they know. And for that connecting person to feel comfortable putting you in touch with their network, they need to have confidence in you. That mediating person is putting his or her name on the line for you, and they'll only do that if you've demonstrated that you are reliable.

5 Embrace the unexpected

A while ago I was on a flight back from Houston. I generally keep to myself on planes, as I often feel nauseated and tired, but this time I was sitting beside a gregarious man who started talking to me. He ended up being friendly and nice, and we had a great conversation. He was a former consultant for a major firm and, as it turned out, we had several acquaintances in common. He added me on Facebook and LinkedIn, followed up with me, and invites me consistently to monthly network meetings he has with people working in consulting across Toronto. It's been an opportunity for me to meet so many new people I wouldn't have otherwise encountered.

Be open to the fact that your network can expand in any way, shape or form. It can grow at a designated networking event, but you can also meet people with overlapping interests at a wedding, while waiting for the subway or on your walk home. Don't close the door to a connection, no matter where you are.

FIVE GOOD RESOURCES

1. Robin Sharma's blog (http://www.robinsharma.com/blog/).
2. *Me 2.0: 4 Steps to Building Your Future*, by Dan Shawbel (Kaplan Publishing, 2010).
3. *Never Eat Alone: And Other Secrets to Success, One Relationship at a Time*, by Keith Ferrazzi (Doubleday, 2005).
4. *The Brand You 50: Fifty Ways to Transform Yourself from an 'Employee' into a Brand That Shouts Distinction, Commitment, and Passion*, by Tom Peters (Knopf, 1999).
5. *Life's a Pitch*, by Stephen Bayley and Roger Mavity (Bantam, 2007).

LISA MATTAM *is widely recognized as a consultant to business professionals across the globe. After almost a decade working in pharmaceutical sales and marketing and strategy both in Canada and the U.S., Lisa founded The Mattam Group, a management firm specializing in leadership, organizational development and strategic process. Under her leadership, The Mattam Group has quickly become an industry leader in talent management; her clients include Pepsi Bottling, IBM, Dell and Bayer. In 2009, Profit Magazine ranked Lisa as one of the top ten women emerging entrepreneurs in Canada. In addition to her MBA from McMaster University, where she graduated as valedictorian, Lisa holds a diploma in European Business from ESC Rouen France.*

6

ADVOCACY
AND POLICY

UNDERSTANDING A government's priorities
is crucial to successful advocacy.

— Sean Moore

⊕ GOVERNMENT RELATIONS

Judy Pfeifer

1 Match your organization's priorities with the government's priorities

2 Be solutions-driven

3 Keep cultivating your relationship with government

4 Form coalitions to strengthen your efforts

5 Build relationships outside government

GOVERNMENT RELATIONS IS the art of influencing which public policy ideas are put into practice. There are government-relations experts who can help and advise you, but ultimately you should be doing government-relations work yourself. The people and organizations closest to an issue should be the ones speaking to government about it. You have the credibility, you have the knowledge, and your words will ring true in a way that no outside consultant's will.

Government relations can strengthen your organization. If you do it well, you can become known as the best advocate for your cause, the go-to person civil servants and journalists call when they need to understand a particular issue better. This builds your credibility, which in turn helps you when you go to donors and ask for money. In fact, government relations draws on many of the same skills as fundraising. If you can pitch a donor successfully, you can be effective at government relations.

1 Match your organization's priorities with the government's priorities

All governments get elected on the basis of a platform, and they generally don't like to veer away from that platform once in office. Go through your government's policy statements and platform to see which elements align with what your organization does. Where can you find overlapping or shared priorities? Those are your entry points in building your relationship with the government. The more you can demonstrate to a government that you understand its aims and concerns, the likelier it is to engage with you.

Let me give you one example. When I worked at Queen's Park, I was chief of staff for the Minister of Municipal Affairs and Housing; one of my areas of responsibility was guiding the development of a policy for the Greenbelt – the region of agriculturally valuable land around Toronto. Protecting that land was a key government commitment. Once local environmental groups saw this was a priority for us, they formed a coalition to help push for the initiative from the outside. They mobilized community groups, they mobilized residents, they supported us in the press, and we worked in tandem to advance the issue. Along the way, I encountered small, neighbourhood-based organizations that joined the coalition and were able to get more attention paid to their own issues because of that. One very small neighbourhood association I remember was trying to fight a highway going through its local park. Because it joined the coalition working on the Greenbelt, that neighbourhood association gained new allies in its own struggle and garnered government attention as well – certainly something it wouldn't have been as likely to do before.

2 Be solutions-driven

Politicians are generalists; they have to know about many things, but they don't have the time to learn about any one of those things in great detail. They don't have the capacity to absorb everything you might know about an issue. So you need to frame your concern in a way that's accessible, that a politician can understand without specialized knowledge, and whose salient details they can remember while also handling 17 other matters at the same time. And then you need to tell politicians what they can do about it. Explain how the government can intervene, and how that intervention aligns with the government's priorities. Governments aren't interested in problems so much as in being able to say they've *solved* problems – so make it clear what the solution is.

Another way of putting it: when you meet with government, have a clearly defined ask. Say, specifically: 'We're hoping for your endorsement of this position'; 'We're asking for this legislative change'; 'Can you support this grant application?' and so on. Be clear, and offer a next step government can take.

3 Keep cultivating your relationship with government

It isn't enough to simply get governments to know who you are – you need to make yourself useful to them. Governments are always looking for information about an issue, and in the aftermath of many government cutbacks, they often don't have the capacity to conduct research themselves. Research is a great service you can offer, a tool that will help you develop a closer relationship with government. (This is what consultants often refer to as 'thought leadership.') If you can bring information to the table and share the insights you've gleaned from the relevant research, you'll be able to develop your relationships with civil servants and political staff. You don't need to commission a 30-page report – 'research' can be as simple as noting the trends you see at your agency, collating basic facts and figures, or compiling recent op-eds and articles about a subject. Governments appreciate seeing these things, and by presenting this information you'll create an opportunity to talk about solutions to the issues you're explaining.

One example of this that you might have seen is the Toronto Community Foundation's Vital Signs report. It's a wonderful document, but it isn't original – it's a compilation of research from other organizations. Every year the TCF holds an event to coincide with the release of the report. Politicians, media and donors are all invited, and have the opportunity to learn more about the findings. And even though the TCF didn't conduct most of the research, the organization's profile has been boosted significantly because it is the one making the information readily available – it is being useful to government.

When trying to get government's attention, also remember that all politics is local. If you're hoping to get a meeting with a certain minister, for instance, find a case that's relevant to your cause in the riding that minister represents. Politicians, ultimately, respond to their constituents; if you can find a local example that highlights the work you do, they will grasp the issue and its significance much more quickly. If you're an agency with multiple locations, first go to the MP or MPP who represents the riding where your head office is located, but make sure you go to the other MPS or MPPS as well.

Finally, if government does what you ask, you need to say thank you. This can be a tricky area, one that organizations often handle poorly. Because your work is never done, it can be tempting to say, 'Thank you for your support so far, but the fight isn't over, we still need . . .' You may be right, in terms of public policy – but that isn't the time or context in which to make your case. Governments are sensitive, especially when it comes to how they are discussed in public. If you've developed a good working relationship, don't jeopardize it by trying to turn these acknowledgements into opportunities to exercise public pressure.

4. Form coalitions to strengthen your efforts

When approaching a policy issue with government, first you need to figure out who will actually be making decisions on that matter. Is it city council? A cabinet minister? A committee? Once you determine who the decision-maker is, work backwards to trace out not just the politicians but key political staff and civil servants involved. Then think of the organizations and individuals who may be able to influence these people. Figure out who, among these influencers, will be supportive of your message – that's where you start building your coalition. Just as important is identifying which organizations are going to oppose you; these are groups you will need to try to bring onside, or to neutralize.

This process is called 'stakeholder mapping,' and you can literally do it on a chart. Divide your chart into the following categories: supportive and informed, supportive and uninformed, informed and unsupportive, uninformed and unsupportive. Once you figure out which organizations and influential individuals go in each quadrant, your aim is to move as many as possible into the realm of supportive and informed. As you work on your issue, this stakeholder map becomes a sort of living document, your way of monitoring the lay of the land.

A key aspect of building this support: use your board members and donors to relay your organization's message. Your board members and your biggest, strongest donors, if they find themselves in situations where they naturally come in contact with government, should be able to have that conversation for you – they should be prepared to reach out as opportunities arise. Similarly, consider recruiting someone with government-relations experience to your board, to boost your capacity to reach out to government effectively.

5 Build relationships outside government

Raising your profile is a crucial part of any government-relations strategy. It's important to be seen: at MPs' and MPPs' town halls, community events, major public speeches and networking lunches such as those hosted by the Canadian Club. The more politicians see you, the more you'll stick in their generalist minds. This can extend to hosting events to which you invite politicians, just as the Toronto Community Foundations does with the Vital Signs report. There's a cost, but it's an engagement strategy that works for the foundation.

There are also some ways to raise your profile by approaching certain constituencies strategically.

The press: Organizations generally know which reporters cover their issues. If you don't know, find out. Call these journalists and try to book meetings, show them your research, and brief them on your work. Your goal is to become part of those reporters' rolodexes. Every morning in every cabinet minister's office, they look at the news clips on their respective areas of responsibility. One of the things they check for: who's quoted and who's not. If you become someone who is consistently mentioned in press coverage, you'll get government's attention too.

The opposition: Working with opposition parties is an essential part of your long-term government-relations strategy as, of course, the party in office will eventually change. But here's the challenge: in working with the opposition, you can't frame an issue or provide information in a way that will lead them to embarrass the current government. At the end of the day, this is a partisan process where 'wins' are cherished by those in government.

There is a difference between applying pressure and using tactics to embarrass. For example, it is reasonable to engage the opposition to challenge government as to why it is not moving on a particular issue. Your goal is to educate the opposition, and to engage subtly with it. Openly criticizing government through the media, or providing the opposition with information the government lacks, could lead to embarrassing a minister. In pursuing this more adversarial route, you'll have created an additional obstacle on your road to success.

Internet presence: Just as with the traditional press, raising your profile online is key to getting noticed by government. Find out who the influence bloggers are on your subject and introduce yourself to them. Get on their radar and give them story tips, just as you do reporters. Government officials increasingly realize that online discussions are bellwethers – early indications of which issues might be about to grip a community, and to which they should be paying attention.

> ## FIVE GOOD
> ## RESOURCES
>
> 1. *The Prince*, by Machiavelli.
> 2. *Why Women Should Rule the World: A Memoir*, by Dee Dee Myers (HarperCollins, 2008).
> 3. *Hardball: How Politics Is Played, Told by One Who Knows the Game*, by Chris Matthews (HarperCollins, 1988).
> 4. *Harper's Team: Behind the Scenes in the Conservative Rise to Power*, by Tom Flanagan (McGill-Queen's University Press, 2007).
> 5. Campaigns & Elections (http://www.campaignsandelections.com).

JUDY PFEIFER *is a vice-president with Hill & Knowlton, where she advises a range of clients on public policy, stakeholder relations and communications. Previously, she was a vice-president at the Toronto Community Foundation, where she successfully engaged the City of Toronto and the Government of Ontario in funding and policy initiatives. Judy has also held the positions of chief of staff to the Minister of Municipal Affairs, manager of corporate issues at the City of Toronto, senior advisor to the Toronto Police Services Board and senior advisor to the Greater Toronto CivicAction Alliance's Greening Greater Toronto project.*

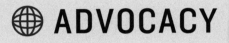 **ADVOCACY**

Sean Moore

1 Understand how
government thinks

2 Undertake do-it-yourself
public policy

3 Build political
capital

4 Be strategically
opportunistic

5 Find your
champions

THE ABILITY TO effectively influence government decisions is a major challenge for small non-profits as well as large organizations. However, there are specific steps non-profits can take to improve their relationship with governments and their effectiveness in lobbying them.

The ideas I suggest here are not about the nuts and bolts of advocacy strategy development or lobbying tactics. Rather, they focus on concepts, approaches and mindsets that can help any organization become a constructive and influential player in public-policy advocacy.

There are several important background considerations. First, our political and public-policy environment is one where we have a substantial and ubiquitous 'argument industry,' comprising sophisticated individuals in the media, academia and interest groups who are well-versed in the art and science of policy and advocacy. For some, it is but one part of their job; for many others, advocacy is their principal focus. This has important implications for those trying to advance a cause – any cause. It it is a crowded and competitive field of activity.

Second, while our public service is one of the most respected, well-educated and (relatively) corruption-free in the world, it is also highly risk-averse and often overworked, in an environment in which demands for attention and resources far exceed the capacity to respond. The public service is also the target of an enormous number of representations – most of them not very well conceived, executed or articulated by either commercial interests or passionate community groups, but all of which take up time.

Third, we live in a society where politics and government are held in low esteem. Surveys and analyses abound about declining trust in all institutions, not just government. For most Canadians, government and politics are 'black boxes.' Seldom, if ever, is there any examination of what goes into government decision making or effective advocacy. To be effective, one needs to delve deeper into the dynamics of policy development and decision making

Fourth, government has to look at issues in particular ways. Public officials usually have a checklist of criteria, policy frameworks and processes that need to be followed in policy and decision making, whether the idea at issue comes from inside or out of government. The elected leadership typically has broad policy positions, a platform on which they were elected, and a myriad of political considerations, all of which will shape its approach to your particular concerns. A common complaint from some interest groups is that 'governments don't listen.' However, advocacy groups are often not aware of their own need to listen, observe and think about what government is confronting. Recognizing and understanding the role and legitimacy of both elected government officials and those in the bureaucracy who carry out the politicians' decisions is key to our democratic system. If you don't understand this, you may find that you are talking to yourself: understanding a government's priorities and ways of thinking is crucial to successful advocacy.

These five ideas are designed to help you avoid common failures in government advocacy.

1 Understand how government thinks

Key to successful persuasion is understanding those whom you are trying to convince: their values, objectives, needs and ways of looking at the world. This is the essential first step in effective advocacy: understanding what government thinks it knows, and why. A process for achieving this is what I call 'strategic inquiry.'

Before you develop your 'ask' (your proposition or request to government), consider how the government – its politicians and bureaucrats – view your particular issue. What are their assumptions, constraints and influences? Your goal is simply to understand both the political and public policy aspects of the issue with which you are dealing.

The six P's of Strategic Inquiry in support of public policy advocacy:

▶ **Public Policy Context**. What is the basic principle – from the government's or decision maker's perspective – underlying the issue you are interested in?

▶ **Process**. Who are the decision makers, what are the processes, and what decision timetables are central to the issue you are dealing with?

▶ **Precedent**. Every decision that government makes is guided by precedent: both previous decisions and setting the stage for future decisions. What are the historical precedents and future implications for your particular issue?

▶ **Positioning**. How is the department/official/politician you are approaching positioned with regards to this issue? How is it linked to their priorities? What language do they use?

▶ **Politics**. What are the interpersonal dynamics (among both politicians and departments) that will affect this issue? Who is interested, and who has an interest? What relationships – alliances, rivalries, etc. – are or could be involved? Who in government could be your champion?

▶ **Perseverance**. Nothing happens in public-policy advocacy unless someone is actively pursuing the issue. Be prepared to spend the time investigating and advocating for your position. Encountering one's first 'no' is usually just the beginning of an ongoing process of learning, rethinking and reframing.

These six P's will help you develop a strategic approach to your advocacy work. They will also provide inspiration for an effective advocacy narrative – the framework that will structure your organization's positioning as you make your case to government.

2 Undertake do-it-yourself public policy

Getting the attention of decision makers and advisors and motivating them to act on what you want is an intensely competitive process. One of the most important things you can do is to provide public officials with material they can use in a format they're familiar with. This involves learning how to 'do' public policy – or at least to know the formats, language and considerations used in government decision-making policy. Most of this information is publicly available on the internet (for instance, in regulatory impact statements) or through Access to Information/ Freedom of Information requests.

To get government to pay attention to your policy recommendations, use its tools and speak its language. Understanding the type of information used by government in its decision-making processes is helpful to any organization that is developing its own strategy to influence public policy. This can provide a blueprint of sorts, one that helps you look at issues in the way those in government are required to. For example, most changes in public policy require a minister's briefing note. If this is the case, provide information in a format that can be used directly in such a briefing note; it will save a bureaucrat's time and may help to expedite the process of moving your issue forward.

To get government to pay attention to your policy recommendations, use its tools and speak its language.

This work can be time-consuming. A government-relations consultant or lobbyist can be of assistance, but often an equally effective alternative is to find a recently retired civil servant who is knowledgeable in the relevant issues and decision-making processes, and may be willing to work on a volunteer basis.

3 Build political capital

Whether its leadership realizes it or not, every organization has political capital. This includes everything from the reputation and accomplishments of your organization and leaders to a supportive membership, network of government contacts and expertise in the relevant area of public policy.

Strategically, the important thing is to view this capital as an asset without which little can be achieved. Building it should be a prime concern of every board whose objectives include being effective in public-policy advocacy.

☞ **Format for a Briefing Note for Public Officials**

Issue (or Subject or Topic – or Purpose, of, for example, a meeting):
A very brief statement of the subject at hand, issue, proposal or problem; ideally, no more than a few short sentences.

Background: This provides the reader with the context that needs to be understood. It usually provides a very short, point-form history of the circumstances that led to the current situation, identifying key players and previous relevant decisions or actions.

Current Situation (or Status): Very brief description of current situation. Summarize options being considered by decision-makers.

Key Considerations: A summary of important facts, developments – everything that needs to be considered now. Keep the reader's needs uppermost in your mind. Substantiate statements with evidence. Double check your facts. Attach additional details as appendices.

Options (also Next Steps, Comments): Basically, observations about the key considerations and what they mean; a concise description either of the options and sometimes their pros and cons or of what will happen next.

Conclusion and/or Recommendations: Conclusions summarize what you want your reader to infer from the BN. Many readers jump there immediately. Make sure any recommendation is clear, direct and substantiated by the facts you've cited.

Key Themes or Messages: This section is added when the briefing note is intended to guide the reader on what points to emphasize, messages to convey, themes to underline

The 'Ask': is there a specific request or proposal being made to government?

(This guide is based largely on a model developed by Professor Susan Doyle of the University of Victoria, Victoria, British Columbia.)

4 Be strategically opportunistic

Machiavellian though it may sound, advocates need to consider the value of being 'strategically opportunistic.' This means aiming for a balance between being reliable and avoiding being taken for granted. Be prepared to be active, but wait for the opportunity where you can have the greatest influence before taking action. Avoid being a one-trick pony: always saying the same things, the same way, demonstrating resistance to change and innovation. Be entrepreneurial; regularly reinvent your organization by offering new and fresh ideas.

Try to be constructive and upbeat. Create a positive communications strategy and reach out – for example, by taking the time to send a note to a particular official encouraging him or her to pursue a certain policy direction. See what opportunities exist for you to take part in policy conversations as they develop. This approach also builds political capital for a time when your organization might have no alternative but to strongly (and publicly) criticize the politician's or bureaucrat's direction. In this way, you can be less predictable but more strategic.

5 Find your champions

The complex, often volatile, nature of political and public policy decision making is such that very little happens with an idea unless there is someone inside government driving the issue forward. The challenge is finding such champions, motivating them and supporting their efforts. Having a champion is a litmus test for your work: if you can't get someone to be your champion, that may be an early warning about the practicality or feasibility of what you're asking for. As one senior bureaucrat told me, 'You may need to ask some questions of and about yourself, your organization, your position or idea, if no one wants to hold your hand.'

The perfect champion is the minister under whose portfolio your issue falls, but don't fixate on this. (Sometimes there can be too much emphasis on getting in to see the minister; in fact, in most jurisdictions, the vast majority of issues are decided elsewhere within government and simply ratified by a minister.) Unless you have successfully made your case with ministry officials and political staff, your chances of success with the actual minister are slim. Political advisors, ministerial assistants, community leaders, area MPs or MPPs, public servants in other departments, and celebrities are all potential champions.

FIVE GOOD RESOURCES

1. Advocacy School (http://www.advocacyschool.org).
2. 'Can Public-Policy Advocacy Be Taught? Or Learned?' by Sean Moore, *The Philanthropist*, Vol. 23, No. 4 (2011) (http://www.thephilanthropist.ca/index.php/phil/article/view/880/745).
3. *Organizing for Social Change: Midwest Academy Manual for Activists*, by Kim Bobo, Jackie Kendall and Steve Max (Seven Locks Press, 2001).
4. *The Democracy Owners' Manual: A Practical Guide to Changing the World*, by Jim Schulz (Rutgers University Press, 2003).
5. *Rules for Radicals: A Pragmatic Primer for Realistic Radicals*, by Saul Alinsky (Vintage Books, 1972).

SEAN MOORE *is the founder and principal of Advocacy School, and one of Canada's most experienced practitioners, writers and teachers on public policy advocacy. Also currently a SiG Fellow and public policy advisor to the Social Innovation Generation collaboration, Sean has more than 30 years' experience in public policy and advocacy related to local, provincial/state and federal government affairs in Canada and the U.S. Sean is a former partner and public policy advisor at Gowling Lafleur Henderson LLP, and has taught graduate courses on public policy advocacy at Carleton University and the University of Ottawa. He has been a faculty member of the Maytree Foundation's Public Policy Training Institute and an advocacy mentor to grantees and fellows of several Canadian foundations.*

$ WORKING WITH GOVERNMENT BUDGETS

Dan Burns

1 Approach government early

2 Develop your relationships

3 Keep the conversation going

4 Review your programs

5 Align with government processes as much as possible

MOST NON-PROFIT ORGANIZATIONS are very familiar with the funding cycles of their donors and granters. Fewer know about government budgets. Understanding the annual cycle of how government ministries prepare and evaluate their spending proposals can help non-profit organizations plan and implement their own activities, and ultimately coordinate these activities to maximize their effectiveness in approaching governments for funding.

☞ **The Annual Budget Cycle**

► **Fall:** Individual ministries prepare an operating plan, including programs, staffing, space and IT for the following fiscal year.

► **Winter:** Ministry budgets are scrutinized in detail, and the Ministry of Finance prepares the overall government budget, including any major program announcements.

► **Spring:** Ministries figure out how to implement their approved budget and allocate the resources they have available.

---

1 Approach government early

Each fall, ministries receive an instruction book with guidelines on how to prepare their budget proposals for the following government fiscal year. (For example, the guidelines might state that the budget must shrink by 3 percent or can include an inflation adjustment of 2 percent). This budget submission does not usually include proposals for new programs or the expansion of existing programs. These are usually considered in a separate process.

Since the maintenance of existing programs may not fall within the instruction-book guidelines, typically budgets include notes on the implications of either maintaining the ministry within the budget guidelines or maintaining existing programs at current service levels.

Agencies should speak to their respective government departments in the early fall, armed with program reviews, assessments and evaluations – ideally including quantitative as well as qualitative analysis and evidence-based outcomes. Recommendations you make at this time could include proposals for making existing programs more effective, as well as proposals for new programs. Ministries would then have current advice from the field as they prepare their submissions

Even in periods of severe restraint, government may still add programs if it is confident the programs will have successful outcomes.

2 Develop your relationships

Ministry budgets are submitted in December or January and scrutinized by central agencies (Cabinet Office, Treasury Board, Management Board, etc.) as the Minister of Finance begins to prepare the overall budget. This budget does not contain the details of each ministry's budget, only the overall spending parameters: tax increases/decreases, major program announcements and total ministry budgets. (The details end up in a separate document called the estimates.)

This is the time when new ideas are normally being sought from outside and within government. If the same idea is heard both in government policy circles and from outside consultation, it has a better chance of penetrating the government decision-making process. During this period, continue a dialogue with your respective ministry, discussing program enhancement ideas and ideas for new programs or the improvement of existing programs. Even in periods of severe restraint, government may still add programs if it is confident the programs will have successful outcomes.

Individual politicians and organizations can have an impact on what is funded during this period. Develop multiple pathways to your goal by fostering relationships with:

- civil servants in appropriate ministries
- ministers' political offices
- MPPS and MPS
- academics
- the premier's 'kitchen cabinet' (i.e., a cadre of unofficial but influential advisors)
- government-relations professionals
- the media

Use contacts developed through your own administrative staff as well as the contacts of your board of directors. Don't rely on one set of government contacts, and always cultivate contacts with a broad range of political stripes. Your organization is in it for the long haul.

3 Keep the conversation going

The government's fiscal year begins April 1; the budget is usually made public sometime between early March and early May. At this point ministries are working within their approved budget envelope to finalize detailed spending for the coming year. As part of this process, they explain detailed budget implications to the non-profit organizations that have requested funding. At this point the ministry may consult with outside associations and agencies about the best use of program funds for the current year.

A well-organized agency or association will be consulting with ministry staff during this period, offering recommendations for the optimal management of program funding. Even if ministries cannot give you their final funding decisions, there is still value in speaking to them about the best use of overall program resources. Explore whether ministries have some contingency funding set aside that allows them to address small program improvements, program rationalization or enhancement, pilot projects or short-term funding needs.

4 Review your programs

Each government normally establishes a timeline for regular program reviews (for instance, at five-year intervals). Extraordinary reviews may be prompted by such things as criticism by the Provincial Auditor General in its annual report, policy changes brought in by a new government, media attention, new fiscal constraints, court challenges, a re-prioritization of resources or a change in federal-provincial relations. In the case of regular reviews, the Provincial Auditor General identifies programs set to be reviewed in February, carries out audits over the summer and publishes the results in November.

A well-done audit produces an insightful analysis of a program's strengths and weaknesses, and a set of recommendations for future development. The ministry responsible for the program in question will then have to spend some time in the fall responding to the auditor's recommendations.

Program reviews by ministries may present an opportunity for a stakeholder organization to present recommendations for program improvement, as well as new program proposals. You can also prepare your own audit, assessment or review of your organization's programs, identifying strengths and weaknesses. If you complete this by Labour Day, this will allow you to work in tandem with the government's own budget cycle.

5 Align with government processes as much as possible

If your organization's fiscal year does not line up with the government funding cycle, consider changing your fiscal year to mesh more closely with it – for example, by moving to a fiscal year beginning July 1. This can be particularly helpful for organizations whose fiscal year is based on the calendar year, and are halfway through their fiscal year before government granting decisions are announced. The same advice applies to strategic plans as well as to reviews of the sort mentioned above.

> ## FIVE GOOD
> ## RESOURCES
>
> While it is always worthwhile to read the governments' annual
> budget and to be acquainted with the estimates for the ministry
> that funds you, you should also have copies of all the ministry
> documentation for your area of work – policy papers, reviews,
> program design documentation, assessments by the Provincial
> Auditor and general communication material.

After a long career as a senior public servant, **DAN BURNS** *now teaches and consults on public policy and public administration, and is active on the boards of a number of public and private corporations. A graduate of Queen's University and the London School of Economics, Dan began his public service career at the City of Toronto's Planning Board in 1975. In 1988 he was appointed Commissioner of Housing, and was responsible for the City's residential land development programs as well the non-profit housing company Cityhome. In 1991 he moved to the provincial public service, and over an 11-year period served as deputy minister in five ministries, including Health and Long-Term Care, and Economic Development and Trade.*

IMPACTING PUBLIC POLICY

Benjamin Perrin

 1 Build coalitions of people
with diverse backgrounds

 2 Identify champions and
opinion leaders

 3 Create and maintain an
effective online presence

 4 Develop focused media and
communications strategies

 5 Be prepared to act at key
moments of change

I STARTED WORKING on the issue of human trafficking a decade ago, when I was in Cambodia – a country in which, lamentably, you don't have to look far to find instances of trafficking and modern-day slavery. It was only a few years later, though, that I realized this problem was manifesting itself (albeit in different ways) in our own country.

What really woke me up to this was a case called Operation Relaxation, an investigation into Calgary massage parlours in 2003. In the end, police identified 43 victims of this scheme, women who had been issued phony credentials and were in the smugglers' power. At the time the case broke open, there was no mechanism for providing these victims with support. Many of them were here illegally, having overstayed the work or student visas they had been issued. In Canada, those who violate the rules of the immigration system are sent to detention and put on the fast track to deportation – and that is exactly what happened to these victims of modern-day slavery.

What did we do in response? At that point, my organization, The Future Group, was busy talking about how to end human trafficking in Cambodia. Suddenly we were faced with this very real issue in our own city of Calgary – and unsure how to have an impact. At a time when victims of human trafficking were being detained and deported, we had no choice but to find a way to tackle the situation.

The biggest roadblock to action on most issues is the evasion of responsibility – people passing the buck. It's especially easy to do that when there are multiple departments and levels of government involved. We determined that 25 different government departments were taking part in a working group on this problem. *Twenty-five*. At working group meetings, it was rarely even the same person showing up from each department.

At the end of three long years, after countless meetings, boxes of documents, and press releases, we were able to help secure some crucial victories: the immigration minister started issuing temporary-resident permits for trafficking victims; those victims were granted basic services, including access to interim health care and emergency counselling; and parliament passed a private member's bill to help tackle a pattern of woefully inadequate sentences for those convicted of child trafficking. Here, based on our efforts to get government to take our concerns seriously and translate them into action, are five good ideas for achieving policy change.

1 Build coalitions of people with diverse backgrounds

Different organizations work in different sectors and have varied constituencies; the more of them you can convince to join your cause, the stronger you will be. You don't have to agree with everything (or anything) else these supporters do, so long as you can sincerely come together on the one issue for which you're advocating. Find that common ground, build trust and establish clear expectations for your partners and your campaign. Long-term coalitions can be difficult to manage, but you might not need one: a targeted, short-term strategy can help you achieve a specific policy objective.

2 Identify champions and opinion leaders

In every organization, including every government agency and department, there will be people who agree with you. Although it may feel like everyone in a department you are trying to bring onside is against you, they are not. As we fought our battles over human-trafficking enforcement, public servants would confidentially say to me: Keep going, we're trying to get a briefing note on this; every time you speak about it, we can say this issue is coming up on the political radar, we need to deal with it, we have some ideas.

A minister may make (or refrain from making) a certain statement; that doesn't mean you're not having an impact. Stay in touch with supporters, and remember that politics moves slowly.

Always keep in mind: the outsiders of today are the government of tomorrow. Career politicians stay in the game for a long time. Get to know who they are, and then get to know them. Take the partisan politics out of it – you need to be able to work with all political parties. Encourage, support and acknowledge those people who help you or show interest, even in small ways. It will pay off down the line.

3 Create and maintain an effective online presence

This may sound like generic advice, but it is critical. If your organization has a web page that hasn't been updated in six months or a year, people will conclude that you're doing nothing, that your organization has ceased operations or gone bankrupt. What you're doing in the real world must be reflected online. One common model is to integrate a blog, which you can easily update with news and commentary, into a larger website, most of which stays static. Facebook or Twitter are also part of the presence you build: these allow for calls to action and can help you mobilize your supporters quickly.

What you're doing in the real world must be reflected online.

Google alerts can be an invaluable source of information and can point you to potential supporters who you might not have known about. Every time someone writes an editorial about human trafficking, I get an alert; the next morning I can call or email the writer and describe what we're doing. That kind of contact is critical.

4 Develop focused media and communications strategies

The days of organizations blanketing the world with a press release and then calling it a day are over. Journalists are stretched pretty thin these days, but they won't just pick a release and publish it. Moreover, if you become known for sending junky or uninteresting press releases, yours will start to get deleted before they are even opened.

If you send a press release, make sure it is about something newsworthy, and that journalists will understand not just what you are saying, but why you are saying it now. Handling media inquiries is not easy – if you can, invest in a spokesperson. Getting media training for your staff, if they'll be dealing with the press, is at least as important. Once you've done that, make sure you know the reporters covering your issues (television, radio, print and online) and get in touch with them. Every reporter has a go-to list of contacts, experts she can call up for comment depending on the subject of her story. You want to be on that list. And don't forget about letters to the editor: they do get read, and they can provide you an opportunity to respond publicly to relevant developments, even if nobody is writing an article that day.

5 Be prepared to act at key moments of change

You don't know when the timing will allow you to implement your great idea, or what role you may play in advancing an issue: no matter your sector or the work that you do, you will always be part of a larger puzzle. That's the joy – and also the frustration – of democracy. Be ready for that moment when it arrives, and keep your sensors on so you can identify it in the first place.

Look for patterns and watch for developments that may pique the interest of others: media will be more likely to report on a story, and supporters more likely to advocate for a policy, if there seems to be a larger trend emerging that requires a response. (In our case: one inadequate conviction could be brushed aside, but several were harder to ignore.)

Be open to everyone and talk to everyone – you never know who may be in a position to help you one day. Do your research and have it available to others in easy-to-digest forms. And when it comes time to make your case, relying on moral or political positions can lead to ceaseless argument but little measurable progress, so look for objective, concrete, indisputable bases for action (in our first case, existing, binding treaties).

FIVE GOOD RESOURCES

1. *The Art of Possible (a handbook for political activism)*, by Amanda Sussman (McClelland & Stewart, 2007).

2. *What Is Policy?* by Sherri Torjman (Caledon Institute of Social Policy, 2005) (http://www.caledoninst.org/Publications/pdf/544eng.pdf).

3. *Memorandum to Cabinet (Templates)*, Privy Council Office, Government of Canada (http://www.pco-bcp.gc.ca/index.asp?lang=eng&page=information&sub=publications&doc=mc/mc-eng.htm).

4. *Writing for Government: How to Write a Briefing Note*, by Susan Doyle, University of Victoria (http://web.uvic.ca/~sdoyle/E302/Notes/WritingBriefingNotes.html).

5. *Taking It to the Hill: The Complete Guide to Appearing Before Parliamentary Committees*, by David McInnes (University of Ottawa Press, 2005).

BENJAMIN PERRIN is assistant professor at the UBC Faculty of Law and a faculty fellow at the Liu Institute for Global Issues. His teaching and research interests include domestic and international criminal law, international humanitarian law and human trafficking. A member of the Law Society of Upper Canada, Benjamin served as a law clerk to the Supreme Court of Canada and has been senior policy advisor to the Minister of Citizenship and Immigration. He was the assistant director of the Special Court for Sierra Leone legal clinic and completed an internship in Chambers at the International Criminal Tribunal for the former Yugoslavia. Benjamin is the founder of The Future Group, a non-governmental organization that combats human trafficking; he served as executive director from 2000 to 2006.

7

GOVERNANCE

GOOD GOVERNANCE is proactive, not reactive:
benevolent neglect is the cause of most
governance problems.

— Tom Williams

MANAGING BOARD– EXECUTIVE DIRECTOR RELATIONSHIPS

Rick Powers

1 Take care of
the basics

2 Be timely

3 Provide
direction

4 Make use of a
consent agenda

5 Record and verify
meeting minutes

A NON-PROFIT'S BOARD has two major functions: supervising management, particularly the executive director, and ensuring that the organization's mission and major goals are being met. The board's function is not to manage the routine functioning of an organization – this falls to executive directors and organizational managers, who are involved in operations on a daily basis.

At meetings, board members must be brought up-to-date on the organization's activities, lest an information abyss develop. The question then becomes: how do we maximize directors' time and value when they attend board meetings?

1 Take care of the basics

The chair of the board and the executive director must collaborate in advance of the meeting to carefully consider what materials are relevant for board members, and to structure an agenda for the meeting. Often the executive director will also provide an executive summary, highlighting what has taken place within the organization since the last board meeting.

An experienced and effective chair is essential for productive board meetings. To assist in the process of identifying which board members might make good chairs, review each director's skill set. If you do not have a natural successor to the current board chair, it is your organization's responsibility to bring in an appropriate board member in a timely manner, and to provide sufficient experience to prepare that member for becoming the next chair.

To encourage board members' engagement, at the beginning of each meeting ask directors to comment on what they have done since the last meeting to further the organization's interests. This will also ensure that your executive director is up-to-date on directors' contributions to the organization. In turn, management should encourage board members to visit the organization's office or to visit a particular service or program. This ensures that the board members know the organization well, which will always improve communications.

Use simple English (or the common language of your group), especially when addressing technical areas. Most people do not understand jargon, so avoid it even at the board level. If you must use jargon, explain the terminology as you go.

At the end of each meeting always leave time for an 'in-camera' session. This allows board members to meet alone, without the executive director and other staff members present. It fosters freer conversation, and is an opportunity to acclimatize new board members who may not feel comfortable speaking out at first. In most cases there are no minutes taken during the in-camera session, unless they are mandated by legislation or practical considerations (for instance, to remind the chair of actions to be taken), in which case the minutes are retained by the chair.

The chair should sit down with the executive director immediately following the meeting (or as soon as possible) to relay what was discussed in the in-camera session. This ensures that the relationship between the board and the executive director is not undermined. Management should not feel disheartened by an in-camera session – often, there will be nothing to discuss and it is simply an opportunity for board members to interact with one another. However, be consistent and incorporate the session into each meeting so it takes place regularly and not only when, for example, there are difficult personnel issues to resolve or performance reviews to complete.

2 Be timely

Most non-profits will stipulate in their bylaws that the board should receive a certain amount of notice prior to a meeting, and most executive directors will book the board for regular meetings well in advance. However, while meetings are often scheduled in good time, the information needed for productive participation in those meetings frequently lags. Board reports and agendas that board members need should be delivered with sufficient time for review: a minimum of 72 hours in advance, and ten days is preferable.

To ensure things run smoothly at the meeting – and as a subtle reminder to directors to read the material that has been sent out in advance of a meeting – the executive director should call the directors a few days beforehand to make sure they have received the relevant materials and to ask if everything is clear. (If a board member has not read the material provided in advance, the chair must be prepared to shut down questions that have already been answered in the background notes.)

Meeting agendas may assign specific times to each agenda item. During the meeting it is the responsibility of the chair to keep the agenda on time.

3 Provide direction

Recognize that the chair and the executive director have more information than other board members, which can influence the direction of board discussion. This is known as 'anchoring' – getting stuck around the information provided by the executive director, chair or another board staff member. This information may be biased in some way or may not provide sufficient context for innovative solutions. One solution is for the chair to designate a board member as a devil's advocate.

Directors must be prepared to ask the tough questions of management to ensure that they have the right information required to make informed decisions.

4 Make use of a consent agenda

Minor decisions that need little to no discussion can be grouped into a 'consent agenda.' The board can review these items in advance and the consent agenda can be dealt with at the beginning of the meeting, saving time for more substantive agenda items. When the executive director calls board members prior to the meeting, it's important to ask if there are any questions about the items on the consent agenda.

How do you determine if the item should be on your consent agenda? Some use the '10 percent rule' as a guide: if an item impacts 10 percent of your budget, it should be discussed as a separate item at the board meeting, otherwise it can be on the consent agenda.

5 Record and verify meeting minutes

Once the meeting is over, draft minutes should be sent to board members within 48 hours.

> ### FIVE GOOD RESOURCES
>
> 1. BoardSource (http://www.boardsource.org).
> 2. Institute on Governance (http://www.iog.ca).
> 3. 'Making Time for Good Governance,' by Doug Macnamara and Banff Executive Leadership Inc., in *Leadership Acumen*, Issue 11, August 2003 (http://www.banffexeclead.com/NewsletterAug03.html).
> 4. *The Best of Board Café: Hands-on Solutions for Nonprofit Boards*, by Jan Masaoka (Fieldstone Alliance, 2003).
> 5. Volunteer Lawyers Service, Legal Health Checkups (http://www.volunteerlawyers.org/gethelp/item.10Point_Legal_Health_Checkup).

After receiving his MBA and LLB from Queen's University, RICK POWERS *worked as a corporate lawyer for Smith, Lyons, Torrance, Stevenson and Mayer (now Gowlings). He later served as corporate counsel for Honda Canada Inc., before joining the University of Toronto in 1992. After teaching and serving in several administrative roles, Rick joined the Rotman School of Management in 2005. He has recently completed a five-year term as the associate dean and executive director of the Rotman MBA and Master of Finance Programs. Rick is the recipient of numerous teaching awards, and his areas of expertise include corporate governance, ethics, business and corporate law, and sports marketing. He is a director of several not-for-profit organizations and frequently comments on legal and governance issues in the media.*

BOARD GOVERNANCE

Tom Williams

1 Good governance is always a work in progress, and particular to an organization

2 Good governance is proactive, strategic, and embraces accountability

3 Manage conflicts of interest early

4 Develop leadership and plan for succession

5 Use them or lose them! Engage your board members meaningfully

GOVERNANCE IS THE process of decision making within an organization. Far too often, organizations pay insufficient attention to the processes they use to make decisions and the changing roles of both the decision makers and those impacted by decisions.

Here are five good ideas for non-profits, all addressing the common challenge of ensuring they have good governance.

1 Good governance is always a work in progress, and particular to an organization

The best governance structure for your organization will depend on its size, culture, age or maturity, and the nature of the service(s) you provide. Look to other non-profits with similar structural features for governance models that can be imported into your own organization.

It is good practice to conduct an annual evaluation of how effectively your organization makes decisions, and how well it implements them. Engaging an outside facilitator to help with this process may be useful. The facilitator does not have to be a professional (and expensive) consultant; he or she can be drawn from a peer organization network.

2 Good governance is proactive, strategic, and embraces accountability

Good governance is proactive, not reactive: benevolent neglect is the cause of most governance problems.

A board that deals with minutiae is a board that does not understand its role. Even a working board must be strategic and look ahead to the next stage of an organization's development. A board does not have the ability to run the organization on a day-to-day basis.

The executive director should present an annual 'state of the union' discussion paper to the board, highlighting changes in the external environment and noting opportunities the board should be considering.

The chair of the board and the executive director of the organization need to have a strong and engaged working relationship. The responsibility for smooth board meetings resides with this team.

3 Manage conflicts of interest early

Organizations tend to get into trouble for two reasons. One is an absence of conflict-of-interest guidelines, dealing with issues such as competitive bids and hiring processes. This really means you must have a well thought out and fully operational plan of board-member education, so both new and ongoing members are aware of their roles and their legal responsibilities while holding those positions.

Far too often conflicts develop between board member and staff because of misunderstanding about the limits of their respective roles.

The other way conflict-of-interest issues can flare up is in the absence of boundaries between personal and organizational decisions. Far too often, conflicts develop between board members and staff because of misunderstandings about the limits of their respective roles. We see board members – often while trying to be 'helpful' – usurping the responsibilities of staff and causing unnecessary tension. This can be avoided by implementing a strong board-member training program and, when slip-ups occur, the board chair having an expeditious and frank discussion with the board member who may have stepped outside his or her legitimate role.

There is a third type of conflict of interest that can arise in organizations with working boards – namely when a key board member is also a key volunteer within the organization. The conflict becomes evident when the board member strongly advocates for the volunteer area in which he or she is involved, which can undermine budget or decision-making processes. In such cases the board chair or executive director needs to be proactive and have a frank conversation with the board member.

4 Develop leadership and plan for succession

Boards can sometimes fall prey to so-called 'founder's syndrome,' when the continual presence of an organization's founder prevents other board members from taking on new and increasing responsibilities within an organization. Eventually, the board becomes fossilized. To prevent this, develop a board policy that limits the terms of office for both board members and those holding executive positions.

The person serving as board chair especially needs prior opportunities to develop skills, understand an organization's culture and be trusted by key staff. Ideally, a board chair will have had experience working as a board member, perhaps as the chair of a board committee.

5 Use them or lose them! Engage your board members meaningfully

The board chair and the executive director are responsible for ensuring that board members are productively engaged. Volunteer time is scarce; if a board member's time is not used well, it will go elsewhere. Therefore, make sure board members are actively engaged in your meeting discussions. Use a process observer – one board member selected at each meeting who is responsible for observing how the meeting unfolds – to report on what's working and what isn't in your board discussions.

In addition, hold focus sessions at least quarterly, organized around a particular issue that is confronting your organization. This gives board members an opportunity to be proactive in shaping the organization.

FIVE GOOD RESOURCES

1. 'How Should Boards Address Conflicts of Interest?' in *Great Boards: the online newsletter for healthcare boards*, Winter, 2003 (http://www.greatboards.org/newsletter/2003/winter/2003winter_GreatBoards_Conflicts.PDF).

2. 'Eyes on Governance: Beyond Board Structure and Committees,' Institute of Corporate Directors, *The Globe and Mail*, November 28, 2004.

3. 'Making Time for Good Governance,' by Doug Macnamara and Banff Executive Leadership Inc., in *Leadership Acumen*, Issue 11, August 2003 (http://www.banffexeclead.com/NewsletterAug03.html).

4. 'Building Better Boards,' by David A. Nadler, in *Harvard Business Review*, May 2004.

5. 'The New Work of the Nonprofit Board,' by Barbara Taylor, Richard Chait and Thomas Holland, in *Harvard Business Review*, September-October 1996.

TOM WILLIAMS is *a professor emeritus in the School of Policy Studies and in the Faculty of Education at Queen's University. He recently retired as the principal of Queen's University where he also occupied such diverse management positions as vice-principal of operations and dean of the Faculty of Education. His research interests are in management development and training, the management of large-scale organizational change, board development in public-sector organizations and means of resolving conflict in public organizations. Tom is a frequent speaker on leadership development and is active as a mediator. He serves as facilitator with a wide range of both elected and appointed boards in non-profit organizations.*

DIVERSIFYING YOUR BOARD

Maytree

1 Start the conversation

2 Develop a board diversity policy

3 Recruit a more inclusive board

4 Create a welcoming environment for new board members

5 Track, monitor and evaluate progress

DIVERSITY IS AN integral part of the Canadian landscape, but the governance of Canada's non-profit and voluntary organizations is not always as diverse as the communities they serve.

Visible minorities and under-represented immigrant communities make up an increasing percentage of our population. Almost half (44 percent) of Greater Toronto Area residents are born outside of Canada, compared to 16 percent of the Canadian population as a whole, and 40 percent of the population are visible minorities. By 2031, visible minorities will be the visible majority in Toronto, comprising 63 percent of the population in the Toronto census area.

A 2010 study of 20 of the largest (based on revenue) charities and foundations located in the GTA revealed that the proportion of visible minorities on boards was only 11.9 percent, compared to 49.5 percent of the area's population as a whole. In addition, four of the 14 charities analyzed, and two of six foundations, had no visible minorities on their boards. This is a missed opportunity.

☛ **Advantages of a more diverse board:**
► ensuring diverse perspectives, which leads to better decisions
► legitimizing an organization's mandate
► building social capital and cohesion among diverse populations
► becoming more responsive to the community and clients
► supporting fundraising and more effective marketing and outreach

Here are five good ideas to make your organization's board of governance more diverse.

1 Start the conversation

There are a number of factors that might cause you to acknowledge a need for greater diversity. For example, you may find that your board's homogeneous composition is limiting its creativity and fundraising ability, or that the demographics of the community you serve have changed. As you consider these and other relevant factors, you can start the conversation on where your organization is on its diversity journey, what changes need to be made and in what order of priority. Remember that becoming a diverse board takes time as well as understanding and commitment from all its members.

Once you and your board are committed to diversifying, consider the following:

- Identify where the impetus to change is coming from: your organization's programming and clientele, staff and/or the board itself
- Explicitly acknowledge the need for diversity
- As board members, be ready to provide leadership on diversity for the whole organization
- Link increasing board diversity to your organization's strategic plan
- Be prepared to break out of your comfort zone – you will be taking risks
- Other organizations have already gone through this journey – learn from them
- Incorporate diversity training for board members into the board's training calendar.

Set aside time at your board meetings to explore issues related to increasing board diversity. A facilitator may be helpful, as it is important for all board and/or committee members to participate fully in the conversation. A lack of knowledge about what diversity means and discomfort with change may make some of your board members reluctant to alter the status quo.

2 Develop a board diversity policy

A board diversity policy signals your commitment to diversity, supports implementation and demonstrates good governance. It will engage your executive leadership to champion the cause and act as catalysts for change, and set the tone for your entire organization.

The development of a board diversity policy may be the function of a board diversity committee or a board governance committee. This board committee can:

- assess the current state of governance practices and identify gaps
- develop draft bylaws, policies and procedures to improve and clarify governance
- recruit new board members
- ensure board orientation and ongoing development needs are met
- ensure committees have a Terms of Reference
- review and make recommendations to the board concerning board composition, size, structures, policies and procedures, bylaw amendments and attendance.

Diversity policies are most useful when they contain the following:

- values statement about the organization's commitment to issues of diversity and equity
- brief statement of the added value that implementing this policy will bring to the work of the board – for example, making better decisions
- concrete statement of objectives
- set of milestones the board would like to achieve
- accountability framework for achieving these
- information on resources to be used to ensure implementation
- accompanying operational plan that outlines, in order of priority, the steps taken to reach each goal.

3 Recruit a more inclusive board

Look at the demographics of your community, the competencies you require and your strategic goals. This will help you prepare to build an applicant pool that better reflects the diversity of the population you serve and that will bring the range of perspectives and experience needed to govern well. You will also have more candidates with experience, knowledge and skills, which will increase the number of qualified applicants who could serve on your board and committees.

Here are a few steps for you to consider:

- Identify what you need and what you have
- Consider your strategic priorities for the next few years – you may have already set these out in a strategic plan
- Identify the skills, experience and knowledge needed at the board level to help you achieve them
- Consider your changing external environment and whether this requires new skills. What gaps will be created by retiring board members?

Develop an outreach strategy that will help you find qualified candidates to fill existing gaps. Structure it so you can advertise for board vacancies in time to screen potential candidates before your next AGM.

There are different models for board eligibility. Some organizations' bylaws state that in order for people to be members of the board, they must first be members of the organization. In this case, you may consider adding a membership drive to your board outreach strategy to increase the pool of applicants you can draw from for your board.

You may choose to include a statement declaring your board's commitment

Look at the demographics of your community, the competencies you require and your strategic goals.

to diversity in the messages you communicate while advertising for board vacancies.

Some outreach techniques include:

- advertising in community hubs and ethnic media, in different languages
- distributing brochures at events and business associations of diverse communities
- advertising in newsletters of ethnic professional or business associations

- reaching out to your volunteer base
- conducting information sessions in diverse communities
- becoming affiliated with services that recruit, screen, and train potential board candidates, such as DiverseCity onBoard.

Finally, design a transparent and clear application process. Ensure that application criteria for board positions are clear and publicly available through board and vacancy profiles. Take a good look at how you manage your selection process now and see if there are any barriers that should be removed so the process is more inclusive. Be sure to leave lots of time for recruiting and selecting new board members.

You now have new board members. What can you do to create a welcoming and supportive environment?

4 Create a welcoming environment for new board members

You now have new board members. What can you do to create a welcoming and supportive environment? This starts with ensuring that meetings are scheduled so as not to interfere with major cultural holidays, that childcare needs are addressed and that venues are accessible.

The following activities are good governance practices in general and are particularly effective in supporting diverse board members:

- Conduct a board orientation
- Have a mentoring program in place
- Offer governance and diversity training
- Keep board members engaged and active.

To be most effective, these activities should become part of every new board member's orientation.

5 Track, monitor and evaluate progress

You have now created and implemented a plan for increasing diversity on your board and for establishing an effective board. You have worked hard to recruit new members with diverse backgrounds and to make board members feel welcome so they contribute their skills, knowledge and energy. How will you know that you have succeeded?

Here are some actions that will contribute to a successful board diversity initiative:

- Link your actions strongly with your strategic priorities
- Clearly communicate what you would like to achieve
- Keep your board diversity plan 'front and centre'
- Integrate your diversity plan into your board decision-making processes
- Allocate resources for implementation of the plan (for example, for a board retreat)
- Put accountability measures in place
- Determine what success will look like
- Measure (and celebrate) progress
- Implement recommendations for improvement.

To track progress, you may begin by going back to your starting point and assessing your board composition against relevant demographic information.

- How have you changed your board nomination and appointments policies and procedures?
- Have your policies and procedures been amended to reduce/ address barriers?
- Take some time to outline what you would like to achieve during an evaluation and how you will go about it. Consider, for example, whether you have the expertise to conduct your own evaluation or whether you will pay someone to assist you.

The success of your evaluation will depend on how well it is planned.

- Think about the scope of your evaluation and set reasonable timelines. Set expectations for the kind of recommendations you would like to see after your evaluation is complete, and think about how you will use your findings.

▶ Determine the outcomes you would like to measure and the indicators that will let you know you have reached your goals. These may be quantitative or qualitative measures.

It is not enough to add new ways of working; we must also remove old systems that reinforce exclusionary practices or expose the values and assumptions that underlie them.

⮞ **FIVE GOOD RESOURCES**

1. Diversity in Governance: A Toolkit for Nonprofit Boards (http://diversecitytoronto.ca/research-and-tools/other-resources/diversity-toolkit/).

2. Replicating the DiverseCity onBoard Program (http://maytree.com/dvcity/onboard/replicating-the-onboard-program).

3. *Diversity Matters: Changing the Face of Public Boards* (Maytree, 2009) (http://www.diversecitytoronto.ca/wp-content/uploads/EN_DiversityMatters.pdf).

4. BoardMatch Leaders (http://www.altruvest.org/Altruvest/boardmatchleaders-main.html).

5. Ten Tips to Diversify Leadership (http://diversecitytoronto.ca/research-and-tools/other-resources/ten-tips).

Established in 1982, **MAYTREE** *is a private Canadian charitable foundation committed to reducing poverty and inequality in Canada, and to building strong civic communities. Maytree seeks to accomplish its objectives by identifying, supporting and funding ideas, leaders and leading organizations that have the capacity to make change and advance the common good. Its policy insights promote equity and prosperity. Its programs and grants create diversity in the workplace, in the boardroom and in public office, changing the face of leadership in Canada. Visit http://www.maytree.com.*

DIVERSECITY ONBOARD *is a governance initiative of Maytree and the Greater Toronto CivicAction Alliance that connects highly qualified candidates from visible minority and under-represented immigrant communities with governance positions in agencies, boards, commissions and non-profit organizations across the* GTA. *Visit http://www.diversecitytoronto.ca.*

FIVE THANK YOUS

GREAT IDEAS are contagious. They spark, build momentum and are carried through to fruition by enthusiasm, dedication and hard work. This book is the result of the efforts and commitment of many.

1. **The Five Good Ideas presenters.** The generosity of the sector's leading thinkers makes this series possible. Not only do they agree to share their thoughtful expertise, they also take time from their busy schedules and commit to a format that makes the series, and this book, an accessible and invaluable resource.

2. **The Five Good Ideas audience.** Their participation at the sessions, provocative questions and enthusiasm to connect with each other are key to building on the momentum and taking action on good ideas.

3. **Coach House Books.** In particular, Alana Wilcox, who had the vision to recognize the potential of this book as a critical resource for the non-profit sector, and Evan Munday for his inventive publicity. Thanks also to Hamutal Dotan, our diligent and committed editor who shaped the presentations into a cohesive resource.

4. **Members of the non-profit community** who provided input at all stages of the book's development. In particular, Chris Reed, Priscila Uppal, Ann Decter, Jeff Dobbin and the outstanding team at Diaspora Dialogues: Helen Walsh, Julia Chan and Natalie Kertes.

5. **Maytree Staff** for conceptualizing, supporting, operationalizing, organizing, filming, transcribing and editing this rich content, all with tremendous care and enthusiasm.

Thank you all for your commitment to making the sector better.

RATNA OMIDVAR *is president of Maytree, a private foundation that promotes equity and prosperity through its policy insights, grants and programs. Under Ratna's leadership, Maytree has been recognized for its commitment to developing, testing and implementing programs and policy solutions related to immigration, integration and diversity in the workplace, in the boardroom and in public office.*

Two recent initiatives have been the Toronto Region Immigrant Employment Council (TRIEC) and DiverseCity: The Greater Toronto Leadership Project. Internationally, Maytree is best known for the Cities of Migration project.

Ratna has been appointed to a number of task forces, including the Transition Advisory Board to the Premier of Ontario in 2003 and to Prime Minister Paul Martin's External Advisory Committee on Cities and Communities. Currently, she is the co-chair of the Mowat Centre Employment Insurance Task Force to examine Canada's support system for the unemployed.

Ratna serves as a director of Greater Toronto CivicAction Alliance (formerly Toronto City Summit Alliance), the chair of the board of directors of TRIEC, and a director of Connect Legal.

In 2006, she was appointed to the Order of Ontario and, in 2010, the Globe and Mail *profiled Ratna as its Nation Builder of the Decade for Citizenship.*

ALAN BROADBENT *is chairman and* CEO *of the Avana Capital Corporation, and founder and chairman of Maytree.*

Alan also co-founded and chairs the Caledon Institute of Social Policy (1992); Tamarack – An Institute for Community Engagement (2001); and Diaspora Dialogues (2005), which supports the creation and presentation of new writing that reflects the diversity of Canada. These and other related organizations create and support civic engagement projects to strengthen the public discourse on civil society, including the Jane Jacobs Prize, which celebrates 'unsung heroes' in the Toronto Region; the Institute for Municipal Finance and Governance at the Munk Centre, University of Toronto; and Ideas That Matter, a public discourse initiative.

Alan is co-chair of Happy Planet Foods, director of Sustainalytics Holdings B.V., a director of Invest Toronto, past chair of the Tides Canada Foundation, advisor to the Literary Review of Canada, *member of the Governor's Council of the Toronto Public Library Foundation, Senior Fellow of Massey College and Member of the Governing Board, Member of the Order of Canada and recipient of the Queen's Jubilee Medal. He is the author of the book* Urban Nation, *and was awarded an honorary Doctor of Laws degree from Ryerson University in 2009.*

Typeset in Whitman, Trade Gothic, Clarendon Text and Knockcut
Printed and bound at the Coach House on bpNichol Lane, 2011

Edited by Alan Broadbent and Ratna Omidvar
Designed by Ingrid Paulson

Coach House Books
80 bpNichol Lane
Toronto, Ontario M5S 3J4
Canada

416 979 2217
800 367 6360

mail@chbooks.com
www.chbooks.com